STRATEGIC INTENT

To
Chuck Wilson
My friend and brother in Christ.
Wishing you all of God's blessings.

STRATEGIC INTENT

Building An Effective Missions-Minded Church

Eric Wilder

iUniverse, Inc.

New York Bloomington Shanghai

Strategic Intent
Building An Effective Missions-Minded Church

iUniverse books may be ordered through booksellers or by contacting:

iUniverse
1663 Liberty Drive
Bloomington, IN 47403
www.iuniverse.com
1-800-Authors (1-800-288-4677)

Because of the dynamic nature of the Internet, any Web addresses or links contained in this book may have changed since publication and may no longer be valid.

ISBN: 978-0-595-50543-2 (pbk)
ISBN: 978-0-595-61553-7 (ebk)

Printed in the United States of America

How many more to the kingdom be sent

If the Gospel was shared with Strategic Intent.

This book is dedicated to my beautiful wife Lolli and daughter Alena, whose constant love gives my life meaning and whose support and encouragement I could not do without.

Contents

Introduction: The Need for Strategic Intent..........................xv

Chapter 1: Assessing Your Missions Program 1

  Assessing your Ministry Team 3

Chapter 2: Building your Ministry Team 5

  Team Recruitment and Qualifications 5

  Team Responsibilities and Delegation 8

  Team Accountability and Procedures 12

Chapter 3: Defining Your Missions Program..........................19

  Mission and Vision Statements 21

  Team Goals and Objectives..23

  Developing a Missions Budget 25

Chapter 4: Investing in Missions 31

  Mistakes to Avoid 33

  A Case for Supporting National Church-Planters 40

  Community Health Evangelism..50

Chapter 5: Ministry Partnerships and Projects 53

  Assessing Potential Ministry Partners 56

  Assessing Potential Ministry Projects..................................60

  Sending Proposals to Your Elder Board 65

  Guidelines for Ministry Partners and Accountability..........66

  Missions Team Responsibilities 69

  Severing Ministry Partner Relationships..............................71

Chapter 6: Ministry Strategy and Planning 73

Increasing Awareness *74*

Increasing Participation *77*

Increasing Support *81*

Celebrating Results *82*

Chapter 7:   Funding Your Missions Program 88

Types of Funding Programs *90*

Presenting Your Missions Budget *93*

Chapter 8:   Creating a Missions-Minded Church Culture 96

Laying a Foundation for Missions *97*

How to Grow Missions DNA *100*

Building a Missions Education Program *101*

Chapter 9:   Missions Outreach 104

Global Outreach *106*

Organizing Short-Term Trips *111*

Local Outreach *119*

Chapter 10:   Defining Success 126

The "S" Factor *131*

Acknowledgments

There have been some incredible Christian people God has placed in my life throughout my walk with Christ, and I have been the fortunate recipient of their friendship, guidance, and wisdom.

To Mel Ramos, who has loved me, taught me, challenged me, comforted me, and been a friend like no one ever before, thank you for placing your trust in me and giving me my first chance to lead a ministry team.

To Harry Brown for your friendship and wisdom, and for allowing me to gain so much valuable insight into the successful church planting process you are a part of.

To David Unruh for being such a wonderful friend and mentor. You truly are a great Christian role model for the rest of us to see.

To Len and Jan Turner for all of your valuable insight into life's challenges and for being such diligent and dedicated prayer partners to so many of us. I cherish your friendship.

To Dave Seeba, Doug McCown, and Don Spears, thank you for allowing me to be a part of your prayer group and for helping me navigate through a challenging time in my life.

To Frank Hawe for your friendship, support, and all of the time you give to so many others for the sake of missions. You have been a true mentor to me.

To Rick Dietzman for your shining example of a dedicated and effective missions pastor. I really enjoyed my time serving with you, and learned so much.

To Randy Easthouse for all of your incredible spiritual insight, for modeling true servanthood, and for the sacrifices you and your family make on behalf of missions every day.

To Mike Lynch and Roberto Alfaro for your friendship and support and for being part of a great global ministry team. It was an honor serving with you.

To Ricardo Ayala for being such a good friend and for all of your support through the difficult times. It was a pleasure leading a life group together with you.

To Gary Strutz for your friendship and all of the personal time you have invested in me. I can't thank you enough for all of your guidance and input throughout the years.

Finally, to God, who makes all good things happen and without whose grace this book would have never been possible.

Introduction:
The Need for Strategic Intent

When it comes to the area of missions, the American church has lost its way. Many churches have no missions program and instead choose to use their money to offer more services to congregational members or to make the church more attractive to nonbelievers. Some churches grow so fast they often overlook or run out of time for this important ministry. A lot of churches that do have missions programs tend to remain the same year after year; they fail to grow and do little to energize congregational members into supporting the program.

Many missions programs are run by faithful, well-meaning people using expensive, outdated methods for sharing the gospel with other parts of the world. There is a tremendous amount of waste and duplication taking place on the missions field, and the tired, old methods simply aren't producing much fruit or exciting congregational members to get involved.

Look at the ministry partner photos on the walls of many churches' entryways and foyers, and you will notice that 50 percent of the supported ministry partners are stateside. Often there is very little accountability or review of ministry partners at home or overseas—once they are supported, they are seldom dropped. There is a general feeling that as long as God has called someone to the missions field and they are demonstrating their faith, they should continue to be supported. It seems quite a few people have forgotten the part about producing fruit. (John 15:8)

I developed the Strategic Intent program with a biblical yet systematic approach to missions that incorporates certain business aspects, including assessment, goal setting, planning, and accountability. God requires us to have faith, but He also has given us gifts, tools, and methods to use for His purposes and to grow His kingdom. The key is to take a balanced approach to missions. I believe God expects us to be both faithful and fruitful.

Every time I give a management seminar, I mention that people have to be good decision makers. This involves having the courage to stand against emotional decision making, which is not always easy. Few people prepare themselves for, volunteer or have a calling for leadership. It tends to be for people who are appointed, because most people are asked to help.

This is true not only in business, industry, and government, but also in ministry. Many people who come into positions of leadership or involvement in churches or missions organizations and committees have little or no training in leadership or management. They are often spiritually qualified but not always very organizationally gifted.

One of the most important aspects of management, especially missions management and stewardship, is the clarity and objectivity that comes from developing and defining vision, purpose, goals, and results. Without guidelines that set parameters and expectations then measure results, organizations and committees are forced to make subjective decisions.

Powerful and transforming things occur when Christian organizations and missions teams use the gifts and tools God has given them. They set standards of excellence and reflect God's high ideals. They clarify purpose and direction. They inspire enthusiasm and encourage commitment. They are articulate and easily understood. They have the ability to concentrate and eliminate waste, and they are ambitious and set goals.

When missions programs are run well, people get excited. They understand the mission, and they want to be involved and share in the blessing. They will knock themselves out to complete the task at hand. Everyone wants to be a part of something exciting. It makes it even more special when people can be a part of something everlasting, because a good program will not only bear fruit, but more importantly, will bear "fruit that will last."

I am often asked, "What makes a missions program successful?" While no two missions programs are exactly alike (nor should they be), there are definitely common attributes that most successful programs seem to have. They are generally structured with guidelines, not rules, that allow the flexibility to respond to changing circumstances and the Holy Spirit's leading while staying true to the designs that God has specifically in mind for them. They are well organized, forward-focused, and enthusiastic about everything they get involved in. And they continuously look for ways to share and promote their ministry.

Successful missions programs are led by pastors or team leaders who are open to new ideas and constantly look for ways to improve their programs. They are well respected and respectful of the members of their team. They are gifted not only with leadership skills, but also the gifts of encouragement and exhortation. Missions programs can't and shouldn't be run by individuals who have been appointed to the position because it needed to be filled. Rather, the leaders need to be naturally excited about missions and possess a genuine heart and understanding for reaching the lost in other parts of the world.

One can learn a lot about a church and its heart for missions by simply walking in and observing what is on hallway or sanctuary walls and what's in the church bulletin. The way video updates are done and announcements are presented gives a distinct feel, too. Churches that have a pulse on missions and a real sense of purpose for what they are doing will find a way to insert missions content into almost everything they do.

You can literally feel the sense of excitement within the congregation. The way church members respond to announcements and what they talk about at church says a lot, too. Even more important are the roles church leadership and the teaching pastor play in the whole picture. Missions-minded pastors find ways to insert missions principles into most of the sermons they teach, giving the church body a greater sense of purpose and understanding for what God desires of them. In those churches, the elders lead or participate on short-term trips, not just pray for them.

A good missions-minded church has high-traffic areas set aside for missions brochures and copies of ministry partner newsletters and photos. The brochures contain everything from budget information, ministry partner information, upcoming projects, and short-term trips to ways for church members to get involved in missions or the missions program.

The weekly bulletin in such a church always contains a section set aside specifically for ministry partner prayer requests, praise reports, budget updates, and special calls for help. The really serious missions churches have bulletin inserts that allow for even greater visibility of the missions program. All information points people to the church Web site, where the missions section can be loaded with unlimited amounts of useful and stimulating information.

These churches take missions to heart. They believe that God has a special purpose for them, and they deeply desire to be faithful to His call. That's what it's all about—helping to bring a change of heart. When the apostles started the first church in Jerusalem, they gave us the model of what a missions-minded church should look like in Acts 4:32:

All the believers were one in heart and mind. No one claimed that any of his possessions was his own, but they shared everything they had. With great power the apostles continue to testify to the resurrection of the Lord Jesus, and much grace was upon them all.

Missions isn't something they pull out of the closet once a year, make a big deal of, then put away again after they fulfill their sense of obligation. They do it all the time. Successful missions-minded churches are that way because their missions program is always out there for everyone to see. They have a "single-mindedness of heart and action" (Jer. 32:39), and they honor God's purposes for them.

That's because God honors churches that stay faithful to His purposes. In fact, He has a special plan and purpose for every church mission program. This is emphasized in Ephesians 1:11:

In him we were also chosen, having been predestined according to the plan of him who works out everything in conformity with the purpose of his will.

The key is to find out what His plan is and then do all we can to bear fruit in those areas He calls us to.

The challenge we face is that too many church members have no global view of Christianity or don't even know what a worldview is. They have no idea who their global ministry partners are or where they are serving. They have no idea how their missions money is used. They have never heard of terms like the 10/40 window, prayer profiles, church planting movements, or unreached people groups. Often, they don't have a good understanding of the Great Commission. Unfortunately, when the once-a-year missions activity is announced, church members stay away in droves, fearing they will be pummeled into feeling guilty enough to support a missions program whose purpose they don't really understand.

Meanwhile, at least one third of the world remains isolated from the Gospel of Christ. According to the International Mission Board Global Research Department, there are still more than 6,500 unreached people groups, representing a population of 3.4 billion, who have never heard of Jesus Christ.

Worldwide, Christians give $270 billion per year. Of that:

$47 billion (17.4%) goes to missions.
$32.4 billion (80% of above total) goes to support domestic missions (12% overall).
$15 billion (20%) goes to support foreign missions (5.4% overall).
Only $54 million (.02%) goes toward mission work among the unevangelized.
(Source: World Christian Encyclopedia, Second Edition 2001. Figures reflect money given worldwide in U.S. dollars.)

American Christians give only 2.6% of their incomes to the cause for Christ.
Only 55% of church missions budgets go to international missions
Only 8% of the international missions budget goes to "frontier" [unreached people] missions.
Of all missions giving, 28% comes from churches, 56% comes from individuals, and 15% comes from corporate donations.
(Source: World Christian Encyclopedia, Second Edition 2001)

The need to mobilize and equip congregations to build better and more effective missions programs that will make a positive impact for the kingdom and glorify God has never been greater. Pastors and missions leaders have a responsibility to help the members of their congregation understand the Great Commission. When Jesus commanded his eleven disciples to go and make disciples of all nations, he also gave them another very important instruction: to teach the people "to obey everything I have commanded you." (Matt. 28:20)

We must help our fellow Christians understand their obligation to grow and continue in the footsteps of Paul and the other disciples, and to help bring light to a dark world. When Paul wrote his second letter to the church in Corinth, he was very adamant about defending his ministry, helping the church understand why he was compelled to be a missionary, and the need for the church to go beyond its four walls to share the Gospel. In 2 Corinthians 10:15–16, he wrote:

Our hope is that, as your faith continues to grow, our area of activity among you will greatly expand, so that we can preach the gospel in the regions beyond you.

He also pointed out how missions should be a natural extension of one's personal growth in faith. Once God reconciled us to Himself through Christ, He committed to us that message. We are now to be His personal ambassadors to the rest of the world. It was all a part of His plan for reconciliation. In 2 Corinthians 5:20, Paul wrote:

> *We are therefore Christ's ambassadors, as though God were making his appeal through us.*

The good news is that God has given every church and missions program a unique missions DNA that is created by His calling on its leadership and congregational body along with a plan to accomplish His purposes. All members of a church body have unique gifts and passions that God has given them specifically, and the challenge is to help them discover what those are and how they can be used for God's purpose. This is especially so with a global ministry team.

The challenge is to build a missions program that taps into that unique DNA in a way that not only builds excitement and participation, but also produces fruit for God's kingdom. When church members witness events, hear stories, or see results of others being blessed, it creates a natural desire to be involved and participate in the blessing. They don't want to miss out.

Many churches don't realize they have a unique missions DNA. Some never take the time to find out what it is, and many simply don't know how to find it. *Strategic Intent* will help your missions team discover its talents, its passion, and its unique purpose in God's kingdom. And it will help you to share those gifts in a way that inspires the church body.

The idea behind this book is to introduce a systematic approach that will help you to achieve God's plan for your team. It can help you whether you are starting a new global ministry or rebuilding and re-energizing a program that has either leveled off, lost its focus, or is experiencing a decline in involvement.

But you have to begin with the end result in mind. The essence of the word "strategic" is that having a plan is important for reaching an intended objective or goal. That plan should include specific elements only if they are considered important enough to affect the achievement of a stated goal.

Strategic Intent is not a one-size-fits-all type of approach. It has been designed so that it can be used for your specific global ministry team. It can be used as a complete program or to address specific areas of need within your ministry. It can be instituted along any timeline comfortable for your missions program. Your team dictates which parts you use and what pace you take through the program.

This book also creates a safe avenue for self-analysis. It will help your team discover strengths they never knew they had. It will also show opportunities for improvement without placing blame. Moreover, it will help you create and foster an environment of mutual respect, trust, responsibility, and accountability within your missions team.

Strategic Intent will help your team and church become more prepared to participate in God's blessings. At the heart of this program is the purpose of helping every missions team become better equipped to be used by God for his purposes to produce fruit for His kingdom. This approach will not only help you increase missions awareness, participation, and support from the congregation, it will also help your church share the Gospel and bless others in a way that others can see.

CHAPTER 1

▼

ASSESSING YOUR MISSIONS PROGRAM

Most people have a natural desire to look forward rather than back. The old saying "You can't know where you're going unless you remember where you've been" really emphasizes not only how important it is to pay attention to and track what your missions program has done in the past, but also how it accomplished it, in order to improve it in the future. Reviewing past objectives, successes, and failures provides the proper perspective needed to make adjustments to set and meet new goals.

Those of you reading this that don't yet have a missions program might be tempted to skip over this section because you don't think it applies to you, but it does. Once you have a program, this section will become an important tool to measure how and if your program is actually meeting the goals it set out to achieve.

Most successful missions teams conduct yearly reviews of their finances and make honest evaluations of their ministry partners and projects, but most teams don't track their results beyond that. While any review is better than none, it is only when you can look at a review of your entire program with respect to the past that you will be able to make a thorough evaluation that helps to identify positive or negative patterns that might be developing.

When I do a review of a missions program, I look at every aspect of the program. I start with the giving history for at least the last five years and measure not only the giving totals, but also the number of individuals contributing. I review the timing of a faith promise campaign or missions festival and its duration. For those churches where the missions program is part of the overall church budget and not funded through a faith promise, I look at the budgeted amount in context with all other church budget items.

Then I look at how the actual missions budget is broken down. I check to see how much is allocated to ministry partners, one-time projects, field emergencies, short term trips, ministry costs, and promotion, and if the team has a contingency reserve for a bad year.

I will cover ministry partners, one-time projects, and short term trips in much greater detail later in the book, but the key here is to measure results, not just faithfulness and desire. How long has each partner been supported, and what gains are they making for the kingdom in actual outreach or conversion numbers? How are they positively impacting the lives of the people they minister to? How does their progress or results compare to other missionaries in the region? If their ministry isn't producing much fruit, is there at least a lot of seed being sown? One-time projects also need to show a positive end result to justify expense. The bottom line is, where are the greatest results being achieved?

If you are sending teams abroad, you must measure their expense against the overall budget, their results, and the long term strategy of the trip in relationship to the entire program. What is the average size of the teams? Are team members new or repeat participants, and how many pastors or church leaders have participated?

If local ministry is the responsibility of the missions team, I look at the budget for local ministries in context of the entire mission's budget, the overall individual involvement, and congregational support for each activity. I then give an honest critique of the results of each of those activities.

Many teams fail to track the frequency of their visible communications with the congregation. But without a track record, you won't have much to go on when you ask for more support from church leaders. They take notice when you can show the actual dates or times you were able to share missions information with the rest of the church body throughout an entire year. This should include announcements, bulletin content, bulletin inserts, videos, guest speakers, sermons, or any kind of special event outside of church Sundays.

Last but not least, it's important to meet with the lead pastor and elder team at least twice a year (preferably quarterly) to get their perception of missions activities. What is the lead pastor's idea of missions in the scope of the whole church? What is the rest of the pastoral staff's perception of missions? Once you have a history and a measurement of current activities, you can begin the process of identifying opportunities for improvement and capitalize on the areas where you already have encountered success.

Assessing your Ministry Team

After assessing the program, it's a good idea to review your team. Does each team member have specific responsibilities and do they understand their roles in the context of the whole team? Are they active participants, or do they mostly sit on the sidelines and show up for meetings and events when it suits them? How do they perform their responsibilities, and can you depend on them? Do you have the right person matched up with responsibilities that are appropriate for their gifting? (This last point is a key issue because ministries tend to be more success-ful when they are built around a person's heart or spiritual gift instead of creating a position that leadership deems necessary but no one wants to take responsibility for.)

Are there areas of your program that you would like to improve but can't because you don't feel you have the right person or people for the job? If so, write them down so you don't forget them. Sometimes God doesn't give us volunteers for areas we think are important because they might not be what He has in mind for your program.

A former pastor of mine once shared his outlook on ministries this way: If God had given someone in the congregation a specific gift and heart to start a ministry, he would embrace it, support this person, and encourage him or her to succeed. But if that person eventually moved away and there was no one to carry on and lead that particular ministry, then he would close it down and focus his support on other areas in the church until God placed someone else in the con-gregation who had a heart and gift for that specific type of ministry.

This pastor's feeling was that you can't effectively force or create any specific ministry unless there is someone who God has raised specifically to start or lead that ministry. He didn't lose any sleep over it because he felt confident in what God intended for his church. That doesn't mean you shouldn't pray for God to raise people up for positions on your team that you think need to be filled; rather, be at peace about it when it doesn't happen and trust God's timing to be appro-priate for His desires.

I would also recommend having at least one team meeting per year that focuses specifically on your team's outlook for the ministry. Have them perform an honest evaluation of the ministry, including your leadership. Lead them through an exercise where they share the hits and misses of the past year. These should be recorded and summarized, with each team member receiving a copy by the following meeting. If you are leading your team properly and have their trust and respect, they should feel comfortable enough to objectively share any concerns they have in a thoughtful and encouraging manner.

Many pastors and ministry leaders fear opening themselves up to possible criticism, but doing so shows the team you have the maturity and desire to continuously improve yourself as well as the ministry, and it will give your team the confidence they need to serve with you. Nothing inspires trust like openness and individual transparency. If your team does identify an area for improvement, ask them to pray for you. In this way you can hold them accountable for their support and prayers.

Take the time to find out more about each member of your team. Do your team members have dreams or desires that God has placed on their heart? Do you? Discuss them and bring them to prayer before God. If you pray as a team and serve as a team, you'll grow as a team. Understanding your team's strengths and weaknesses will help you discover and develop a roadmap for your ministry to follow.

Finally, take the time to learn how the rest of the congregation views the missions program—not just the missions diehards, but the rest of the church body. Do they have a basic understanding of your team's ministry? Can they relate to it? Do they feel comfortable with your stewardship of their (God's) money? Find out what forms of media they respond to. The more connection points you can create, the better. Ask members of the church body to critique the missions program. You will be amazed at the response when you encourage the input and involvement of others.

CHAPTER 2

▼

BUILDING YOUR MINISTRY TEAM

Team Recruitment and Qualifications

As I stated in the beginning of this book, few people are prepared for or volunteer for leadership positions in ministry. It tends to be a calling for people who are appointed because most people are asked to help. Many people feel intimidated when asked to serve and afraid they might fail if they take on an unfamiliar responsibility. That is why it is so important to get people to serve in areas where their true passions can come to the surface.

A good ministry team should be comprised of people with various gifts, talents, abilities, and personalities that will actively participate in the growth of the ministry. They should possess a genuine heart for God's plan for the world and have a heart to utilize their gifts and passions to advance God's family worldwide. Sadly, some people don't think they have been blessed with any gifts. Sometimes it just takes a nudge and some encouragement from a ministry leader to help them discover what these gifts are and apply them to the ministry's goals. A good leader is one who sees what other people don't see in themselves.

The key when selecting volunteer leaders is to let them know the scope of their responsibilities to the team, and that you will support them and help them succeed in that responsibility. Most of the high attrition rate in volunteer positions in churches can be attributed to disappointment from unmet personal expectations, responsibility in an area of ministry they have not been properly equipped for, burnout from too much responsibility with not enough leadership or spiritual support, or a failure to understand the time commitment needed to accomplish the task at hand.

Note that "lack of necessary skills" is not listed above. That is because most volunteers are more than capable of growing in their responsibilities—God sees to that. The apostle Paul says as much in Philippians 2:13:

> ... for it is God who works in you to will and to act according to his good purpose.

The key is for your team members to be united in one purpose, supported and empowered by you to achieve the goals that God has for your missions program.

Many recruits quit or fail because they don't properly understand what they are getting into—because ministry leaders don't properly prepare the recruits when they are considering the position! If they need to be available for a two-hour meeting twice a month for most of the year, with additional meetings or time as needed for special missions events, let them know in advance of their decision. If they need to give four to eight hours minimum per month working on a particular scope of ministry, tell them before they take the position.

Don't schedule team meetings without a clear agenda. A number of times I have seen ministry leaders ask their team if they want to meet without even having an agenda. This frustrates the doers on the team because there is no real sense of leadership or direction. Other times, a leader takes advantage of volunteers, exhorting them to put in double time because of a new goal the leader has created, or because the leader is so unorganized they have fallen behind and need to make up for lost time. This places an unfair burden on members that are already trying to deal with the pressures of life and responsibilities to their families and jobs.

Proverbs 11:25 says:

> A generous man will prosper; he who refreshes others will himself be refreshed.

A worship pastor friend of mine once told me that it didn't matter how successful a ministry team was or what goals they achieved if the team was unhappy or didn't get along well with one another when trying to achieve those goals. He said "Eric, never forget—it's all about the people. If you support and encourage them, they will trust you and work together as a team, working in unity to obey the plans God has laid out for your ministry."

A successful ministry leader understands that people are not all alike and each team member might serve a different function. In fact, a successful leader specifically looks to create balance on the team and isn't afraid to try and find it. Romans 12:4 says:

> *Just as each of us has one body with many members, and these members do not all have the same function, so in Christ we who are many form one body, and each member belongs to all others. We have different gifts, according to the grace given us.*

Your task is to make sure all the parts of the team function in unison. You know the old saying:

Together

Everyone

Achieves

More

Paul said something similar in 1 Corinthians 12:24–26:

> *But God has combined the members of the body and has given greater honor to the parts that lacked it, so that there should be no division in the body, but that its parts should have equal concern for each other. If one part suffers, every part suffers with it; if one part is honored, every part rejoices with it.*

Your ministry team may be about saving the lost and serving the poor, but it should also serve as a ministry to one another.

That said, you also have to be willing to speak to a team member who might not be meeting his or her responsibilities and commitments or is being disrespectful to you or other members of the team. Perhaps there is a personal or family problem that requires you to minister to this person. Perhaps they are being distracted by other desires or commitments, or their interests have changed but they are afraid to tell you. Whatever the cause, it's your responsibility to address that person's actions or inactivity and do what's best for the team.

Ultimately we have the responsibility of serving a God who desires fruitfulness in us. He not only chose us to do a job, but to do it well, because when we are fruitful, we glorify God. Jesus taught his disciples in John 15:16:

> *You did not choose me, but I chose you to go and bear fruit—fruit that will last.*

Being a disciple of Christ comes with a responsibility that requires producing fruit; it's a responsibility that we are given when we are saved. Put simply, it's a job requirement.

Sometimes volunteers just need some time off for spiritual refreshment. It is important as a leader to recognize that need and suggest a break to someone without their having to fear they will lose their position on the team. I know of some churches that make it mandatory for volunteers on ministry teams to take a break from ministry every three years, for a period of three months to a year, to ensure they get some quality time for spiritual renewal. I would argue that a policy like that isn't needed if leaders are in tune with the needs of those they serve alongside.

Team Responsibilities and Delegation

As with any job, there should be a detailed description for each position. Potential team volunteers deserve to know what the purpose of the ministry is and how it functions. I usually recommend creating a simple "Ministry Overview" document that describes the functions of the ministry team and how it operates.

You might want to start by explaining how the missions program fits in with the overall goals of the church and what the primary roles of the team are. Is your goal to be a sending church or a partnering church? There's a big difference, and we will explore this subject in greater detail later. If your focus is to be a sending church, explain how you plan on growing church members who feel they have been called into the missions field. Explain the team's role in helping to prepare those individuals to be ready for field work.

If you are a partnering church, explain how the team goes about selecting and maintaining a relationship with its ministry partners and how the team will educate and inform the rest of the church family about who they are and how they serve. Explain your ministry partner review procedures, and if you don't have any, develop some! (More on that subject later) Potential team members should have some idea of how you select new ministry partners.

You need to explain how the team searches for opportunities to invest in strategic, one-time missions projects around the world that will help advance the kingdom of Christ. Are the projects evangelistic or holistic in nature, or a combination of both? Will the team also be looking for opportunities to invest and participate in local outreach?

Most missions teams operate under the oversight and approval of an elder board or church leadership. But if it is the responsibility of the team to create, monitor, and maintain the budget of the missions program in relation to the funds you receive, say so. Whether you operate from an annual faith promise program or a percentage of the church operating budget, let them know.

What about short-term missions trips? What's their purpose within the context of your particular congregation? Explain how you seek and provide oversight for short-term missions trip opportunities. Is the primary purpose to help support current ministry partners and investigate ministries that might become potential new partnerships, or is the primary purpose of short-term trips to build a heart for missions within the congregation? It's something to think about.

Are all team members expected to actively participate in the annual church Missions Festival, staff the monthly missions table, and regularly attend and participate in Global Ministry Team meetings? The entire team should be involved in setting goals and strategy for the missions program, and they should be encouraged to participate in or lead short-term missions trips.

There are a number of ways to delegate responsibilities with your team. The key is to think about the end result you are trying to accomplish and create job descriptions that give you the greatest chance to achieve success. Consider breaking down your ministry team into specific areas or departments that specialize in a particular area of ministry. Then break those down further into supporting roles. Each member should have a specific responsibility within one of those departments and possibly play a supporting role in another.

A Ministry Organization Chart could look something like the ones below, which are from the last church I served at before I moved to Idaho. The first chart below was in place when I came on board the missions team and included local community outreach; the second is the one that I developed with Mel Ramos, our Pastor of Advancing Ministries, to make our ministry more effective for our particular program goals.

Missions-Minded Church
Original Ministry Organization Chart 1

EDUCATION/AWARENESS

Outreach—seeks and implements ways to involve MMC in the world—Adopt-A-People, Sister Churches, etc.

Missions Projects—seeks opportunities to fund projects, liaison to missions agencies, project feedback

Missions Education—missions classes, Kids-on-a-Mission, Web site, bookmarks

Ministry Partner Profiles—provide congregation with ministry partner information, (i.e., ministry focus and strategy)

COMMUNICATION

Missions Updates/Results—bulletin inserts (prayer requests and praise reports), calendar of events
GMT Promotion—actively promote missions and ST trips through banners and posters, coordinate announcements
Ministry Partner Oversight—coordinate effective review process, complete with summaries
Special Events—missions breakfasts, short-term trip team recaps, guest speakers, etc.

MOBILIZATION

Short Term Trips—ensure budgets are set and met, coordinate with team leaders, guide and support
Ministry Training and Preparation—team and trip preparation, post trip download, individual field preparation
Prayer Ministry—create and maintain life group missionary prayer network, short-term trip prayer network
Missionary Care—host missionaries, transportation needs, life group visits, filling emergency needs

LOCAL OUTREACH

Food/Clothing Closet—collection of food and clothing, coordinate involvement in Operation Christmas Child, etc.
Community Events—self explanatory
Specialized Ministries—sports ministry, prison ministry, hospice and local outreach
Church Planting—create cell churches and sister church plants

New Ministry Organizational Chart 2

MINISTRY ADVANCEMENT

Ministry Partners—seeks and coordinates strategic partnership opportunities in targeted countries
Missions Projects—seeks opportunities to fund projects, liaison to missions agencies, project feedback
Ministry Partner Oversight—monitor progress and coordinate effective

review process, ministry focus profiles

Strategic Programs—seeks and implements ways to involve MMC in the world with other churches (Adopt-A-People Group, Sister Church programs, information sharing, and church partnerships)

SUPPORT and DEVELOPMENT

Budgeting and Finance—monitoring financial condition of ministry to maintain fiscal accountability

Resource Development—fundraising, faith promise, corporate sponsorships, calendar of events

Promotion—actively promote missions and ST trips through banners and posters, coordinate announcements

Special Events—missions breakfasts, short term trip team recaps, guest speakers, etc.

MISSIONARY CARE

Missionary Care—host missionaries, transportation needs, life group visits, filling emergency needs

Prayer Ministry—create and maintain life group missionary prayer network, short-term trip prayer network

Ministry Partner Communication—maintain two-way communications and coordinate prayer needs

Ministry Updates/Results—publish bulletin inserts for prayer requests and praise reports

MINISTRY MOBILIZATION

Missions Education—missions classes, Kids-on-a-Mission, Web site, bookmarks, men's and women's ministries

Short-Term Trips—ensure budgets are set and met; coordinate with team leaders, guide and support

Ministry Training and Preparation—team and trip preparation, post trip download, individual field preparation

Ministry Opportunities—coordinate and promote personal investment opportunities for congregation (Disaster Relief, Christmas Catalogs, Adopt a Child, Food for Hungry, Compassion Intl., etc.)

There are different values to both charts, and I need to stress that there is no one-size-fits-all chart. It should be configured based on the strengths and weaknesses of your team and the goals that God has given you a desire to achieve. It should also be reviewed every few years to make sure the structure still has maximum effectiveness and to make adjustments if needed.

When this church was smaller, the global ministry team was responsible for both local and world outreach. But as the faith promise program grew, so did our responsibilities, and eventually it was decided to separate them and create a new independently led local ministry team, which in turn allowed our team the ability to focus more specifically on world missions.

Team Accountability and Procedures

An organizational chart allows you to have greater accountability from your team. It eliminates gray areas when it comes to individual responsibilities because it is available for everyone on your team to see. (Everyone on the team should have a personal copy of the chart.) It also makes it easy for potential new team members to see your areas of need and pray about what position they might fill.

As a ministry leader, you need to create a good balance within your team between members fulfilling their personal responsibilities and supporting the rest of the team. Team members need to realize they have an obligation to the team and to God to fulfill their responsibilities, support each other, and build one another up so the ministry can succeed. Paul taught the church in Philippi a great lesson in unity in Philippians 2:1–5, and I would encourage you to share it with your team:

> If you have any encouragement from being united with Christ, if any comfort from his love, if any fellowship with the Spirit, if any tenderness and compassion, then make my joy complete by being like-minded, having the same love being one in spirit and purpose. Do nothing out of vain conceit, but in humility consider others better than yourselves. Each of you should look not only to your own interests, but also to the interests of others. Your attitude should be the same as that of Christ Jesus.

To help keep your team on track, it is important to attach achievable completion dates to all projects. When it is a team project, agree as a team on a completion date. When it is an individual's responsibility, agree together on a completion date and hold that person to it. Give them the support or tools they might need to succeed, but then hold them accountable. If it's a long project, make sure to obtain updates on a regular basis to keep the project on track and guide them through any rough spots.

Although it might sound like it, the goal here is not to place all the emphasis on your team's completion of their assigned tasks. If the only motivation is completing tasks, then they will be missing out on the major potential blessing of a change of heart. Completing tasks becomes a matter of heart when team members realize the importance of their mission; the salvation of lost souls is at stake. Your goal is to foster an environment that creates in their hearts a desire to please God, and although they have a responsibility to the team to complete their assigned tasks, their ultimate motivation should be to participate in God's blessing.

This goes for praying over decisions as a team or with an individual, too. Set a deadline in order to avoid hearing that old standby for not reaching a decision, "I'm still praying about it."

Set a date for all of your team decisions. Depending on the urgency of the problem or decision, you may need to suggest something like, "Let's pray about this for the next week to discern what God is saying and make a decision on the fifteenth."

Often I'll hear team members say, "God isn't saying anything to me yet." I think this happens sometimes because we aren't always specific in our prayers. Many times people pray general prayers like, "God, please show us what you want us to do," or "God, please let us know your desires," instead of being specific and asking Him things like, "Heavenly Father, we are lifting this specific question up to you and ask for your hand of approval on it. If it is your will please show us; if it isn't, please close the door."

Sometimes God yells back at us loud and clear, but we can't hear Him because we are so busy concentrating on our own desires or getting distracted by life in general. That's why there should always be time set aside for group prayer. Jesus taught his disciples in Matthew 18:19–20:

Again, I tell you that if two of you on earth agree about anything you ask for, it will be done for you by my Father in heaven. For where two or three come together in my name, there I am with them.

Now I am in no way making light of prayer, because it is the foundation for everything in Christian life and ministry. But often prayer is used as an excuse to delay action, not make decisions, or get anything done. These teams are gripped with paralyzing indecision because they lack the faith to complete the task at hand.

In the book of James, we are taught the practice of Christianity, and in Chapter 2, James teaches about the balance between faith, action, and deeds. He insists that if we are to have real faith, we can't have one (faith) without the other (deeds). He teaches in James 2:14 and 17:

> *What good is it my brothers if a man claims to have faith but has no deeds? ... In the same way, faith by itself, if it is not accompanied by action, is dead.*

He goes on to say in James 2:22:

> *You see that his faith and his actions were working together, and his faith was made complete by what he did.*

Faith, by its very nature, must be tested in order to be experienced. The bottom line is: do your homework, discuss it, pray about, and get it done!

Many global ministry teams are scared to make mistakes for fear of losing God's favor. While stewardship should always be taken seriously, sometimes God lets us make mistakes so we can learn from them. Now, repeating mistakes is another matter altogether, but if you and your team have taken the time to pray about a decision and have done your homework, but the results don't meet goals or expectations later on, then trust that God allowed it to happen. Use that experience to improve on future practices. After all, "If you wait for perfect conditions, you will never get anything done"! (Eccles. 11:14; NLV)

When things do get done on time, the team or an individual achieves their goals, or a project is successful, congratulate them and let them know how pleased you are. The author of Hebrews said it best in 10:24:

> *And let us consider how we may spur one another on toward love and good deeds.*

Consider taking the team off-site occasionally for a time of reflection and celebration. Most important of all, make sure to thank and praise God as a team for the way He has used you to achieve His purposes.

It's also important to hold team members accountable for attending team meetings and staying for the entire duration. Occasional business and family scheduling conflicts are one thing, but if meetings are held on a regular schedule or are rescheduled based upon approval of the entire team, then there shouldn't be any reason to miss them or leave early. After all, if you made the basic schedule known to each team member before they accepted a position, then there shouldn't be any surprises.

Make sure you have an agenda for every meeting and send it out at least one week in advance of the meeting. Ask for additions to the agenda to be made within 24 to 48 hours of the original sending. Try to structure meeting agendas so they follow the same format each time. For instance you could break it up as follows:

- Team Prayer

- Previous Meeting Minutes Approval

- Budget Update

- Ministry Partner Updates

- Project Updates

- New Proposals

- Communications to Church Body

- Team Member Status Reports

- Short-Term Trips

- Promotions

- Local Ministry

- Additions to Agenda

Your agenda should be created so that it stays within the agreed-upon time frame for meetings. It's better to place fewer items on an agenda and complete it by the end of a meeting than to cram it so full that you only get through half of it, which can leave team members frustrated. I would also suggest that you set aside specific meetings for strategy and planning sessions and don't include these items in the agenda for a general meeting. The agenda should always include the minutes from the previous meeting.

Having a healthy set of team guidelines and creating an agenda for meetings are not the only important policies for allowing team leaders to run things smoothly. It is also necessary to have clearly defined parameters that prevent the business-type team members from becoming frustrated with the spiritual-type team members and vice-versa. In the end, all team members will become unhappy from the lack of progress that results from inconsistency. It's really important to understand the difference between the various members of your team and get them to work together.

There is often a huge difference between the world of business and the rest of the mission community. When someone in the business world goes from the pace and risk of business into the culture of a typical church ministry team, they sometimes suffer a tremendous shock. They no longer find the discipline of the marketplace, which holds businesspeople constantly accountable for their decisions. Many times they don't see any urgency from the team in the pursuit of easily measured goals. And if they don't have a strong leader, they also don't see a healthy insistence that all team members consistently contribute some tangible value to the ministry. This is very important in order for them to have a healthy respect for team leaders and fellow team members.

On the other side of the coin, you have the deep spiritual thinkers who like things warm and fuzzy, and who often use feelings and spiritual revelations to replace the analysis and strategy of the businesspeople as the guideposts for their decisions. They tend to consider the methods of the businesspeople on the team as harsh, insensitive, or, at a minimum, out of place with the more spiritual side of the team.

Now I'm not in any way suggesting that Christian business people aren't spiritual. I'm just trying to highlight the two different mindsets that you need to be aware of. Again, it all comes down to a matter of heart. The challenge is to help your team master an understanding of each other and help them work through results that might not always meet their expectations. The goal is to strike a balance between patient spirituality and disciplined action—otherwise, you risk paralysis.

When you do hold meetings, it's important to have quorums and decision standards. When I joined the missions team at my first church, they had a policy of requiring a unanimous decision on all proposals in order for them to pass and be approved. While this type of thinking can be considered "high reaching," it often results in gridlock or issues being permanently tabled because one team member refuses to change or accept the opinion of the rest of the team. In essence, the requirement for a unanimous decision can be used as a form of veto power by any individual team member. For many teams, a simple majority isn't a good enough confirmation, either. It allows a few members of the team to push something through when the rest of the team is absent.

Unfortunately, politics do exist in churches (even though they shouldn't). I suggest having the team operate like most business-world boards and adopt a minimum quorum standard and then a specific majority vote standard. At my first church, we had nine members on our team, so we adopted a policy of needing at least five members to establish a quorum. Then we set a 2-1 vote ratio for our vote standard. That meant that with nine members present, we needed a minimum 6-3 vote to pass a project; eight members 6-2; seven members 5-2; six members 4-2; and five members a 4-1 vote to pass a proposal. It was amazing how much more we accomplished.

Finally, try to avoid being a committee and become a team or a ministry instead. Keep in mind how the rest of the church membership might view your team. Most people's impressions of committees tend to be negative because committees are viewed as authoritative boards that argue and discuss things then make decisions that they expect other people to implement. Many lay people get nervous going in front of a mission's board or committee for fear of their ideas or proposals being ridiculed or turned down.

Ministries, on the other hand, tend to be viewed more positively because they minister to the needs of others. Ministries are perceived as actually doing things. They serve and care. That makes members of the team more relatable to the rest of the church members because the ministries all work together to support the congregation.

Encourage or even require team members to become involved in at least one other church ministry. At a church I used to attend, one of our pastors always encouraged everyone in the congregation to serve in one and a half ministries. He suggested that everyone should lead or participate in one ministry that God had called them to and play a supporting role in another. In this way, church members were exposed to other areas of ministry, which helped them not only to grow but also to appreciate what others did in the church.

The other benefit from this level of involvement is that if you are a missions person, it gives you the opportunity to serve with other members of the church and not only share your heart for missions with them, but also show you care about and appreciate the work they do in the church. The more people sense that missions team members are for the whole church, the more likely that the rest of the church will be supportive of missions.

Some members might feel overwhelmed by this request, or you as a missions pastor or team leader might feel your team will be over-committed by getting involved in other ministries. If that's the case, ask yourself in what other ways the members of your team rub shoulders with the average church member, who you want to see support and be involved in missions.

Many pastors or team leaders want their team members to commit themselves completely to their particular ministry or missions program, but what ends up happening is that team membership becomes somewhat exclusive and a missions subculture develops in the church. Pretty soon, you'll start to hear people say things like, "It's one of those missions weirdos," or "It's an event for missions people."

When this happens, you lose the potential for expanding your base for missions support because you have no relationships with church members outside of the missions crowd. People have to know you care before they will listen to what you have to share. When we are solely focused on missions, we run the risk of losing perspective on what is important to others in the church. The goal must be to build a sense of community, and community happens when there's a sense of relationship and celebration.

CHAPTER 3

▼

DEFINING YOUR MISSIONS PROGRAM

Throughout the world, thousands of people die everyday without ever hearing the Good News of Jesus Christ, and therefore they die with no chance of getting to heaven. When Jesus taught Nicodemus, He was very specific:

I tell you the truth, unless a man is born again, he cannot see the kingdom of God. (John 3:3)

Just to make sure Nicodemus got it, He stated again in John 3:7:

You must be born again.

When Thomas asked Jesus, "How can we know the way?" Jesus answered in John 14:6:

I am the way and the truth and the life. No one comes to the Father except through me.

Yet, if you talk with the average Christian, many still believe that there must be another way for nonbelievers to get to heaven. They will say things like, "I'm sure God wouldn't forsake someone who doesn't know Him," or "God is a good

God; He isn't mean to people." Or even, "I'm sure if they're good people and work hard, God will take them up into heaven."

It's their way of reconciling God's judgment and mercy. This mindset leads to a general lack of urgency in the minds of many Christians to share the Gospel with those in other parts of the world who haven't had the chance to hear about Jesus. Unfortunately, many missions programs have this same general lack of urgency. They operate in a way that makes them feel comfortable, even if what they are doing isn't producing much fruit.

This is wrong; we need to be better stewards. God expects us to take up the Great Commission to expand His kingdom, and He expects us to manage the financial resources He has provided to fulfill His calling. With that responsibility comes accountability, which is determined by the combination of what one knows and what one actually does with that knowledge. It's a relationship of insight and obedience. You can't fulfill God's purposes for your ministry while focusing on your own plans or staying in your comfort zone.

We need to build a new sense of urgency, a sense of mission in the hearts and minds of average Christians. Quite simply, we need to transform the culture inside the church so we can impact the culture outside the church. We have to help our fellow Christians understand that God loves and cares for the entire world, not just our little corner of it. Anyone in the world has the possibility of coming to Christ, but only if they find out who He is, and only if we care enough to share. Jesus taught Nicodemus this principle in John 3:16 when He told him:

> For God so loved the world that he gave his one and only Son, that whoever believes in him shall not perish but have eternal life.

God emphasizes the world many times in the Bible and in many ways. We are just a small part of it. We must do a better job of helping followers of Jesus understand the very important responsibility they have in it. We must also help them be more aware of the needs of those less fortunate than us, the ones who don't have the same opportunities that we do. God expects us to help the poor and disenfranchised of the world and to be a voice on their behalf. In fact, we have an obligation to help our fellow man. Proverbs 31:8–9 says:

> Speak up for those who cannot speak for themselves; ensure justice for those who are perishing. Yes, speak up for the poor and helpless, and see that they get justice.

It is important that Christians understand this. Why? Because the more Christians are involved in helping the poor, the more credibility we have in being their advocates and the more effective we can be in helping to address their needs.

When we help meet their needs, they become more receptive to the saving message of Jesus Christ.

The need to mobilize and equip our congregations and to build better and more effective missions programs has never been greater. We need to get more people involved in the task of missions. The good news is that God has given every church a unique DNA and a plan to accomplish His purposes. The key is to find out what that plan is for your church and then stay faithful to that plan.

Mission and Vision Statements

If you are building a new ministry team, you have to have an understanding of what God might be calling your team to do. This can only be accomplished through group and individual prayer. If you are going to rebuild your ministry team, you have to re-evaluate and redefine why you exist. Enduring ministries have clear plans for how they will advance the Gospel. They are equally clear about the sense of purpose they have and the values they will always stand for.

Fortunately for us, God has given us specific instructions on gaining wisdom in order to understand his plans for us in Proverbs 2:1–6:

> *My son, if you accept my words and store up my commands within you, turning your ear to wisdom and applying your heart to understanding, and if you call out for insight and cry aloud for understanding, and if you look for it as silver and search for it as hidden treasure, then you will understand the fear of the Lord and find the knowledge of God. For the Lord gives wisdom, and from his mouth come knowledge and understanding.*

While a ministry's practices and strategies should always be open to change; its core values and purpose should not. This is what is called core ideology, and it defines a ministry's enduring character. It can be viewed as the glue that holds the ministry together as it grows and develops, and it comes from seeking the will of God for guidance and inspiration.

Your ministry should have a core purpose; this should become your mission statement. To be effective, it should reflect the team's idealistic motivations for doing the ministry's work, and it should capture the soul of the ministry. The core purpose itself should never change; rather, it should inspire change in the way you do things. Now, you might say that your church already has a mission statement. But unless your church is a missions-minded church down to its core, your team should have its own mission statement that defines its primary objective. A missions statement explains why we exist and what we are trying to do.

At Silver Creek Church Community, our mission statement was: "We exist to strategically support ministries and projects, around the world and locally, in order to reach people across the barriers of language and culture with the life-changing message of Jesus Christ. We will strive to maximize the impact of all people called to participate in missions within the Church, so that we as a body may fully utilize all of our gifts to further God's purpose."

You should also have a scriptural purpose that supports the mission statement you have created. The scriptural purpose of Silver Creek Church Community's involvement in missions was:

1.) To fulfill the Great Commission. Matthew 28:19–20

2.) To share Christ's heart for the world. Matthew 9:36

3.) To obey Christ by confessing Him to the world. Matthew 10:32–33

4.) To prayerfully send out and support workers into the world's harvest. Matthew 9:38

Once you have addressed your core purpose, you need to decide how you are going to achieve it. This is where a vision statement is needed. It should be fairly simple, yet clearly define how you plan to reach your goals and the methods you will use to achieve them. Our vision statement at Silver Creek was: "To create an effective Missions Program through increased awareness, participation, and support, in an infectious (exciting) and nurturing environment that enables everyone to have a part in the Great Commission."

Last but not least, your team should have a team slogan that clearly says what you do and that anyone can understand. Your team slogan should be brief and to the point, memorable, and define in a nutshell what your ministry team is all about. Think about who or what you are trying to reach, serve, change, or impact. What is your ministry team working toward or trying to build? Is your ministry about bringing, helping, sharing, or winning?

My last ministry team had the responsibility of both local and global outreach, yet we approached each part differently. We tended to serve our local communities, but we were also doing our part to reach the world for Christ. Our team slogan became, "Serving Communities, Reaching the World."

As with everything else, a team slogan should be rooted in and supported by scripture. Every ministry team should have a team scripture that reflects the overall purpose or goal of the team. Is your team focused on equipping or preparing members to serve on the missions field? Is your team about sending people to do good works and deeds? Is your team focused on bearing fruit, blessing others, or glorifying God?

You might say that your team is about doing all of the above, and it tries to address all of these areas of need. And it should strive to. But every team has a particular strength that comes to the surface based on the gifts and spiritual leadings of its members. All efforts should flow from these strengths. This exercise is about being in tune with the Holy Spirit. It's about focusing and defining who the team is and how it can best bring glory to God.

Team Goals and Objectives

Now that you have your sense of purpose defined, we need to look at the goals or objectives global ministry teams should have to help you fulfill that purpose. Team goals should be divided into two segments, internal objectives and external objectives. The internal objectives focus on what your team needs to do in order to build support within the congregation. The external objectives focus on what your team needs to do in order to be more effective on the missions field.

The objectives below are goals that all teams should strive to incorporate. You might find more that you want to add, but these should serve as a starting point to creating your own.

Internal

1.) To educate and encourage the congregation about the role and importance of missions in the lives of all mature Christians and encourage participation in global ministry.

2.) To support people whom God has called to long- or short-term missions service and missions-related activities, giving them opportunities to serve according to their gifts.

3.) To give church members a greater focus and feeling of ownership of those ministries where the team has a major investment and personal involvement.

4.) To give the missions program the greatest amount of visibility and publicity possible so that more church members are exposed to the needs of the world around them.

5.) To create ways to nurture outside diversity for missions ideas coming to the missions team.

External

1.) To strategically focus primarily on unreached people groups and those parts of the world with little or no available Christian witness.

2.) Create and nurture specific ministry partner relationships that would enable greater involvement and knowledge of missions with our congregation.

3.) To adopt an unreached people group by the congregation.

4.) To give the congregation opportunities to participate in neighborhood improvement projects that help them to develop a heart for serving others.

5.) To give the congregation opportunities to serve on strategic short-term trips that meet a specific need and help them develop a heart for reaching the lost.

All of your planning and everything the team strives to do should be looked at as series of strategic goals that leads to series of defined results:

To help the unaware become aware by capturing their attention.

To help the aware become interested by appealing to a felt need or personal value.

To help the interested become concerned through an emotional encounter.

To help the concerned become involved by giving them opportunities to act.

To help the involved to serve through opportunities to pray, give, participate, and mobilize.

Setting goals and objectives is all a part of proper planning. There's an old saying, "Plan your work and work your plan." The Bible says it another way, in Isaiah 32:8:

But the noble man makes noble plans and by noble deeds he stands.

Spend time planning with your team and put your plans in writing. You won't regret it.

Developing a Missions Budget

One of the most overlooked aspects for many missions programs is the ministry budget. Some teams have no idea what their budget is or how much money they have to work with at any given time. Some teams actually do divide their budget into different areas, but because of poor planning, they take money away from one area to cover a shortfall in another. That's like robbing Peter to pay Paul. Can you imagine the confidence this might inspire in your ministry partners (let alone the congregation) if they ever found out?

Most budgets should include budget categories such as Ministry Partners, Ministry Projects, Emergency Funding, Short-Term Trips, Ministry Costs, a Contingency Reserve, and Local Outreach (if it comes under your program's responsibilities).

Ministry Partners: This part of the budget should go directly to the monthly support of your ministry partners and nothing else. You should consider creating a preset support limit for new ministry partners for their first year of support to give you time to see if their ministry is bearing fruit and to review how well they communicate with the team. Funding for ministry partners should be based on actual faith promise pledges or set church budgets, not wishful thinking.

Ministry Projects: This part of the budget should help fund strategic, one-time missions projects (beyond your ministry partners) that will have an immediate impact for God's kingdom. This could include training and equipping church planters, purchasing materials and equipment used to support mission's efforts, or international disaster relief.

Emergency: This should be used for urgent requests from your ministry partners above and beyond their regular support and could include items such as medical emergencies, vehicle repairs, or a shortage of supplies. (Some teams prefer to have international disaster relief funding come out of this part of the budget.)

Short-Term Trips: Provides additional funding support for members of your church who participate in church-sanctioned, short-term missions trips. This could go toward travel expenses, travel documents, trip immunizations, trip supplies, or ministry tools that might be used in the field. The only time this fund should be used to pay completely for someone's trip is if the trip was deemed necessary by the team or church leadership to send someone to support an existing ministry partner or investigate a potential new one.

Contingency Reserve: A reserve should be established in case your Faith Promise funding or church budget support drops below the projected amount needed to support your monthly ministry partners. Unless your church suddenly experiences a large drop in members, this fund should not exceed 10 percent of your overall budget. A reasonable reserve will be understood by most people, but if the missions funds become too protected by the committee, it will create a stumbling block when future appeals to raise money are made.

Ministry Costs: This part of the budget should cover costs incurred by your team during the fiscal year, such as ministry promotion, supplies, education, communication, and missions awareness. You should strive to keep your overhead low. On the other hand, investing strategically in greater visibility of the program usually leads to higher returns in financial support and increased involvement of the church body. In order to be fiscally responsible and get the congregation's funds to the missions field, this part of the ministry fund should generally not exceed 5 percent of the overall budget.

Local Outreach: The funding for local ministry, if under the oversight of the missions team, should definitely be separated from the regular ministry projects fund so expenses can be tracked independently.

Assign a percentage amount to each part of the budget and stay within the guidelines of the budget. It's okay to adjust the percentage weightings of the budget at the beginning of each new budget year if you see the need or if there is a change in ministry direction, but it's best not to change the budget midseason.

If you have funds left over at the end of the year in addition to your contingency reserve, I would recommend that you shift those funds into either Ministry Projects or Local Outreach. Outside of one-time special gifts, you shouldn't use excess funds to increase monthly ministry support to partners because you can't guarantee that you will be able to maintain that increased support the following year.

If you have a fairly large overage in your budget at the end of a fiscal year, it may be a sign that you or the team wasn't as diligent as they should have been in finding missions investment opportunities. Some missions teams are filled with indecision for fear of making a mistake with God's money. But God honors those who faithfully and diligently seek his purposes:

> *And without faith it is impossible to please God, because anyone who comes to him must believe that he exists and that he rewards those who earnestly seek him.* (Heb. 11:6)

To seek God's will and trust your decisions to Him is the very essence of faith.

Being entrusted with investing God's money is a great responsibility and shouldn't be taken lightly. But do you really think God would have made you responsible with his money if He didn't intend for you to do something with it? Sometimes you have to take an occasional risk in order to be successful. Look at the Parable of Talents. The successful servants were the ones who proved their faithfulness by taking risks that produced fruit (Matt. 25:14–30). If you have done your homework, no investment should be too risky.

Accidents and mistakes are a natural part of life. There is usually a reason for them and God uses them to teach us and help us grow. Look at David's words in Psalm 37:23–24:

> *The Lord delights in the way of the man whose steps he has made firm; though he stumble, he will not fail, for the Lord upholds him with his hand.*

All of us stumble from time to time, but if we have been diligent in our research and placed our decisions before God (prior to making them) and have truly taken the time to seek His will and listen to Him, then He won't let you down.

If you are at a smaller church with a smaller missions budget, you might want to consider having preset spending limits for one-time ministry projects. This prevents you from putting all of your eggs into one basket, especially if the investment doesn't bear much fruit. As your program and budget grow, you should either raise these limits or eliminate them; otherwise, you are creating a barrier to God's work and His desires.

The first church I ever attended had a congregation of more than two thousand members and a mission's budget of over $400,000. They had a preset spending limit for one-time projects of $10,000 that had been created when the missions program had first been established. It had served them well when they had a smaller missions budget, but they had not updated their policy in fifteen years.

Shortly after I joined the missions team, a nonmember of our church wrote a half-million-dollar check (yes, you read that right) specifically to our missions program. Our team didn't know what to do with the money. The older, more experienced "guardians" of the committee were so scared to make a mistake that by the end of the first year, we had only spent $50,000 of the gift. They were proud of the interest we were earning at the bank and thought they were being good, conservative stewards.

I tried to share a good business investment approach, which in its simplest terms boiled down to, "nothing ventured, nothing gained." But it fell on deaf ears. To make matters worse, I was the least experienced and youngest Christian on the team. Some of the team agreed with me, but the rest dug in their heels. I knew nothing short of scripture would sway them, and perhaps a strategic project that we could participate in.

It all comes down to attitude. In missions, we must have an attitude of trust in God, not an attitude of fear. Let's look at Jeremiah 17:7–8:

> *Blessed is the man who trusts in the Lord, whose confidence is in him. He will be like a tree planted by the water that sends out its roots by the stream. It does not fear when heat comes; its leaves are always green. It has no worries in a year of drought and never fails to bear fruit.*

God doesn't plant trees that don't bear fruit.

Sometimes it's not a matter of fears that impede us, but rather the barriers we place in front of us. The author of Hebrews taught about removing barriers and pursuing God's goals for us:

> *Therefore, since we are surrounded by such a great cloud of witnesses [your team], let us throw off everything that hinders and the sin that entangles, and let us run with perseverance the race marked out for us. (Heb. 12:1)*

This finally got the team to start thinking.

The juicy project came next. One of the missions agencies we partnered with was working with an Iraqi national (prior to the overthrow of Saddam Hussein) to build and establish the first Christian school in Iraq. They had a great plan and even had the support of the government itself because it would allow for the children of government officials to attend the school and receive the type of education they so highly coveted, even though it would expose their kids to Christianity.

Our end of the project came with a fairly high price tag for us, one that was way beyond our then-current artificial support limits. After a few months of team discussion and prayer, God knocked that barrier down and the project was approved. The funding amount approved was absolutely precedent-setting for the church at that time, but the investment paid off. Seven years later, the school is still standing, children are coming to Christ, and parents are coming to Christ through their children.

After that, the wall came tumbling down. Many more and larger projects were approved. We didn't hit home runs with all of them, but the congregation started taking notice when we shared reports and lives were changed. It also opened the door for a complete review of the ministry budget and the way our team operated. That was a very good thing.

Once you have a budget, you should share it with the congregation. It lets them know you are open to scrutiny, that you don't take them for granted, and that you care enough to share it with them. After all, it's their money! This will help them understand how the team operates, and it will give them more confidence to entrust their money to you. You don't have to show every line item, just the percentage breakdown of the different funding areas and the general types of things those areas contain. Here is an example:

Missions-Minded Church
Global Ministry Budget Explanation

There are a tremendous number of ministries in the world helping fulfill the Great Commission, and we receive many requests for supporting these ministries and the projects they engage in each year. As a means of being equitable about support requests, a filter has been created by the Global Ministry Team (GMT) based on the level a region of the world (or a people group) has been reached by the gospel. Those areas where there is little or no gospel witness (e.g., Africa, Asia, Indonesia, and the Middle East) or that are strategic in nature are given a higher priority than those areas where there is a strong gospel witness (Europe, South America). This helps us decide which request for support will be accepted and at what funding level they will be supported.

These requests are collected throughout the year. Each request is discussed and prayed over, and a group consensus is reached. The requests are then sent to our church leadership for their approval. It is our belief that we have a partnership with those we support. This means we have regular correspondence with our partners, visits to Missions Minded Church when possible, and financial updates. This helps us decide whether or not future support will continue.

Funding for missions is made possible by your pledges and participation in our Faith Promise. All of our missions funding is based on the total amount of pledge cards turned in on "Missions Sunday" (the last Sunday in March). Of all Faith promise funds, 85 percent go directly to support our ministry partners, missions projects, and sending short-term teams to the field. The current financial breakdown the GMT has established is as follows:

50% Ministry Partners: This part of the budget goes directly to the monthly support of our ministry partners.

15% Ministry Projects: This part of the budget helps fund strategic, one-time missions projects (beyond our ministry partners) that will have an immediate impact for God's kingdom. This could include training and equipping church planters or purchasing materials and equipment used to support mission's efforts or international disaster relief.

10% Emergency: This is used for urgent requests from our ministry partners and could include items such as medical emergencies, vehicle repairs, or covering a shortage of supplies.

10% Short-Term Trips: Provides additional funding support for members of MMC who participate in church-sanctioned, short-term missions trips.

10% Contingency Reserve: This reserve was established in case monthly ministry partner support drops below the projected amount.

5% Ministry Costs: This part of the budget covers costs incurred by GMT during the fiscal year, such as ministry promotion, supplies, education, communication, and missions awareness.

I would encourage you to create a once-a-year bulletin insert and a Web page along these lines outlining your missions budget and how decisions are reached about how the money is used. The more informed your congregation members are about how their money is invested, the more comfortable they will be investing in your missions program. It's an equation of their trust, your respect of their money, and the ability to produce results with their investment.

CHAPTER 4

▼

INVESTING IN MISSIONS

Many teams do a good job of budgeting and maintaining the financial side of their missions program, but do a poor job of investing in areas where the Gospel has yet to be heard. That's because many missions teams do a poor job of discerning where God really wants them to be and opt instead to invest in areas where they are most comfortable. Too many teams invest in areas of the world that have already been reached with the message of Christ or in areas where there is a tremendous amount of ministry duplication. That is why we still have so many people groups who have yet to hear the Good News.

The country of India, for instance, receives a lot of funding attention, but much of the missions effort is in Southern India around Bangalore and Hyderabad, where there is a fairly large Christian movement already in place. It's the Silicon Valley of India and, compared to the northern part of the country, is more comfortable to live in, with more modern conveniences. Naturally this is where most of the Western missionaries and short-term teams go. Very little funding goes toward supporting national church planting ministries that reach out to Northern India.

The problem is that India is a mostly Hindu country, and a basic tenet of Hindu culture is to pray to many gods—the more the better. People in essence "collect" gods with the idea that the more gods they have and the more times they pray to them, the more secure their afterlife will be. To many Indians, Jesus

Christ is just another God to pray to, and many Indian nationals make confessions of faith to multiple ministries and missions workers.

Yet ministry agencies all document these confessions of faith independently, which skews the figures of how many new believers there actually are. This happens when you have too many agencies reaching out to the same people in the same area. They feel good about the numbers of converts they are getting, report the results to congregations back home, and everyone celebrates. But no one can understand why there isn't a larger transformation taking place.

The apostle Paul spoke out about this very problem in his second letter to the church in Corinth when he wrote in 2 Corinthians 10:16, "For we do not want to boast about work already done in another man's territory."

So where in the world should your missions team be involved? Where should it invest? I created a list of the fifty most unreached countries in the world and asked our team to review the list and pray for thirty days, asking God which five countries He wanted our team to invest in. At the end of the month, we gathered together, and each of us shared our list of five countries. It was agreed upon ahead of time that if any country was mentioned more than once, it would automatically make the master list. My goal had been to come up with ten countries, and that is exactly what we came up with.

There are many sources with up-to-date information on missions activity in every country. I have created a list of some pretty good sources that is available on my Web site, www.strategicintent.org, that might be helpful. You don't have to base your team's prayers on the fifty most unreached countries; it's just a suggestion. You could instead pray about any five countries God places on your heart and go from there. Or if you and your team feel led to be involved in a specific region of the world, pray about countries (preferably unreached) in that region.

While having a strategy will help your team be more focused and organized, it should still be flexible enough to respond to the Holy Spirit's leading when a region of the world is experiencing a revival and funding could help discipling in that area. You should also give consideration to countries based upon the culture inside your church. People do want to feel like they are making an effort and impact within their own culture. This can be a more difficult decision, though, if your church body is made up of people from a mostly reached country or culture.

In that case, consider strategic one-time projects in a particular region that can make an immediate improvement in the lives of those that live there. Perhaps there's more of an emphasis on quality of life projects in those areas like building, feeding, or medical programs that show the love of Christ to an already reached country, and less on evangelism. This allows you to focus most of your long-term support on areas that still haven't heard the Gospel.

I would always try to encourage cross-cultural missions as much as I could. It's good for the congregation to learn about people outside of their comfort zone and to develop a heart and compassion for the rest of the world. The bottom line, though, is that your ministry should be driven by your team based on God's leading, not from agencies or missionaries who are looking for support. This doesn't mean you completely ignore a proposal in an area you haven't selected; it's just given a much lower priority. If you do your homework and seek projects in areas God has called you to, you'll find plenty of great opportunities.

Mistakes to Avoid

Some teams invest in the right areas, but in ministries or missionaries whose methods are outdated and not producing much fruit. My first church had an American couple who had spent fifteen years in the field trying to reach out to Muslims in Kenya. Our church had heard they were having problems, and their field reports were somewhat lacking in content. Prior to my joining the team, our church sent a member of the missions committee to Kenya for a week to see if there were any problems and to witness their ministry first hand. He came back and reported that all was well; although they were indeed struggling, he felt they were being faithful to their call and doing the job God had called them to do.

A few years later, I co-led an Impact Team on the missions committee whose areas of oversight included Africa. The couple had come home for furlough, and it was the task of the co-leaders to meet with them and get an update for their ministry. The first question I asked after the usual greetings was, "So, how many people have come to Christ as a result of your efforts this past year?"

They looked at me dumbfounded and said, "What do you mean, this past year? We're reaching out to Muslims."

I glanced at my partner and then asked, "Okay, how many Muslims have come to Christ since you have been in Kenya?"

The husband thought deeply for moment, looked over at his wife and replied, "Well there was that one guy about twelve years ago."

His wife interrupted him and said, "Yeah, but honey, I think it was the Baptists that led him to Christ. He just attended our Bible study for a while."

They gave it some further thought and agreed, "Perhaps one or two."

I nearly fell out of my chair! With complete puzzlement at this point, my co-leader and I said, "Describe a typical day in your life and what you do."

The husband replied, "Well we wake up, we pray for a while, we go to the market and go shopping, we mingle and talk to people, and we invite them to our once-a-week Bible study at our home."

So I asked, "How many people come to your Bible study?"

The wife replied, "We don't get very many, but we did have six once."

"What happened to them?" I asked.

And she replied, "We don't know."

At that point, my co-leader and I asked in unison, "What do you do the rest of the week?"

The husband replied, "Prepare for the Bible study."

We couldn't believe what we were hearing! Perplexed, my co-leader said, "Tell me, are any Kenyan nationals coming to Christ?"

They replied, "Oh yes, in droves!"

The last thing I asked them was, "Do you have any idea how this looks from our end?"

They replied, "Yes, I guess not too good, but after all, our calling is to reach Muslims."

I couldn't help but think to myself, *Are you sure?*

This couple had been supported by our church at $900 per month for fifteen years! Here we were, $160,000 later, with nothing to really show for it. The problem wasn't so much with this nice, faithful, disillusioned couple. They hadn't really done their homework, and they selected an extremely poor missions agency to operate under, which did a very poor job training and preparing them and gave them very little oversight, encouragement, or help along the way.

But our church was not without fault. We never contacted the missions agency to attempt to intervene on behalf of the couple. We also failed to do anything when we recognized this couple was not cutting it on the field. The committee member who visited them a few years earlier didn't understand the need for both faith and fruit. Even more disappointing was the fact that it took the committee close to year more after our report to finally make a decision to end funding support for this couple.

After spending a year on sabbatical stateside, immersed in the study of Muslims, this "career" missionary couple is now being supported again. They are stationed in England and reaching out to Muslims in a group setting with other "career" missionaries under the same agency.

Does this mean you shouldn't be sending any homegrown missionaries overseas? Absolutely not, but churches must be thorough in their background checks and research and much more prudent and strategic in their decision making.

There are many wonderful pioneer missionaries from the United States that do an incredible job reaching out to unreached countries. Many are moving from pioneer work to becoming trainers of national church planters and are very much needed in the missions field.

What I am suggesting, though, is that when your church has a choice between supporting a missionary in an unreached country as opposed to a reached country, invest in the unreached country. Many times, where a missionary desires to serve is not the place where there is the greatest need. The reason we have so many Western missionaries working in countries that have already been exposed to the Gospel of Christ is because so many churches continue to support them.

If that support were removed, they would be forced to either get a secular job and do outreach with their own funds, or they would have to consider working in a country that actually needed their talents to share the Gospel where no one had heard it before.

Some people will argue with my emphasis on devoting more resources to reaching the unreached versus reaching out to countries or areas where the Gospel has been well known for ages but where attendance is low. After all, much of the New Testament is comprised of letters to Churches in an attempt to get them back on the right track.

Let's look at a country like England, for example. For several centuries, it produced, and still does produce, some of the most dynamic pastors preaching around the world. There are probably more Bibles per capita owned in England than any other country in the world, yet the churches there are alarmingly empty. Except for funerals and occasionally weddings, few churches fill more than 10 percent of their seats on any given Sunday.

Or look at the Netherlands, which gave us Calvin and some of the most prolific missionaries in history, next perhaps only to England. There are more devout atheists than Christians in the Netherlands. Germany is not quite as bad, but the land of Luther has almost as many devout Muslims as Christians and as many atheists as both. In fact an argument could be made that there is definitely a need to reignite the fire of Christianity throughout Europe in formerly Christian nations that are rapidly succumbing to atheism, agnosticism, and Islam.

There is a temptation and belief by many that we need to rebuild the Church among the formerly Christian nations first, so as to have a solid base from which to spread the Gospel. This is why we have such a disproportionate amount of missionaries and missions agencies still operating in Europe instead of unreached countries. While I don't want to diminish the efforts of people working in reached countries, the fact is, those countries are indeed considered "reached."

In order to complete the Great Commission, we have to reach all people groups, not all people, and that is why I'm trying to throw more focus on those areas. In Matthew 28, Jesus said, "therefore go and make disciples of all nations or peoples." There is an emphasis on reaching nations and peoples (note the plural) not to make disciples of every person for Jesus to return. This is backed up in Mark 16:15–16, when Jesus commands his disciples to "preach the good news to all creation. Whoever believes and is baptized will be saved, but whoever does not believe will be condemned."

Jesus already knows that not all who hear the Gospel will accept Him. The people of England and many other countries of Europe have been exposed to the message of Christ; they just don't accept Him and have turned away. Unfortunately, they will have to deal with God's judgment when the time comes. Jesus instructs his disciples in Matthew 10:14:

> If anyone will not welcome you or listen to your words, shake the dust off your feet when you leave that home or town. I tell you the truth, it will be more bearable for Sodom and Gomorrah on the day of judgment than for that home or town.

This is an example of modern-day England or Europe, and to some extent South America. All we can do as Christians is share the word, but if it is rejected, shake the dust off our feet and move on to places that are open to the teachings of Christ. Trying to reignite a passion for Christ in Europe is like trying to force something to grow in barren ground. You have to sow where the soil is good and harvest where the fields are ripe. The Parable of the Sower in Matthew 13 explains this well.

There are thousands of churches in England and Europe and South America with good pastors at the helm. Sending more missionaries over isn't the answer. These are actually very strong sending nations. The people in those countries have had the opportunity to hear the Gospel of Christ, while people in unreached parts of the world die every day without ever getting the opportunity to go to heaven. And that is our responsibility.

We have to make an effort to share where the word hasn't been heard yet. The added benefit is that a former Hindu or Muslim that converts to Christianity has a much better chance of being accepted when reaching out to Hindu and Muslims in England or Europe than a Western missionary does. The same can be said with a former Buddhist in Japan, China, or Korea. The trust level and openness is just plain different. There is a high probability that they will in fact eventually be the ones that re-evangelize white, Anglo-Saxon Protestants and lead them back to Christ, too.

The same is already happening in the United States. We now have more than 2,300 missionaries from other countries reaching out to their former nationalities and religions and sharing the Gospel. It's a reverse form of evangelism, but it is taking hold here in America. It's hard for Americans to grasp because we are so used to being the ones that make things happen. The future of missions is going to be very interesting and much different from what it was in the last century.

So it becomes our responsibility to encourage potential missionaries to go where they are most needed, not necessarily where they have a desire to serve or where they feel the most comfortable serving. This can be a tough message for someone who has a burning desire to serve overseas to hear. We also have to respect and honor the fact that if the Holy Spirit has placed a burden in some-one's heart to reach out and serve a particular country or culture, it is not our place to question that heart or douse the flame they have burning inside of them. It is our responsibility to help them consider how they might reach out to the country or culture that God has planted in their heart. Proverbs 19:21 says:

Many are the plans in a man's heart, but it is the Lord's purpose that prevails.

A person does not necessarily have to become a missionary to serve or support a particular country. They could go on a short-term trip with a specific purpose to address a need in that area. They could become a prayer warrior for that country or get a job in that country. They could financially support existing ministries already reaching out and doing work in that country. They could engage in fund-raising work. They might become a spokesperson for that ministry or people group and work to make the congregation (and others) aware of the need to support those doing the work. They could also help to coordinate supplies to ministries working in that area—there is a host of other nonmissionary work to do.

At my last church, we had a couple from a local church solicit our global ministry team to support their new ministry. He was American and she was from Mexico, and God had placed a burden in their heart to work in a small village in Central Mexico. This couple had no coverage with a ministry agency, no experience, and no training, but their home church was "sending" them to serve—in a village that already had existing Christian churches planted and reaching out to the region.

They appeared to have a plan to make more progress than the existing churches had, and in a shorter amount of time. After a fairly lengthy and divided debate, our team decided to support this well-meaning couple for a small monthly amount on a one year trial basis. The experiment was an absolute failure.

When the couple tried to implement their unproven methods, they were rejected by the local people. They had a hard time working with the other "national" church leaders in the area because they were viewed as competition for their congregations. When the dejected couple looked for guidance, they had no missions agency to minister to them, lead them, or give them a boost of encouragement.

You see, they had never really researched the existing political church climate to see if they would be bringing a new or valued dynamic into the area. They also didn't know if their ministry plan was actually different from the other existing churches, let alone even compatible with them. Even though the wife was from Mexico, this couple didn't fully understand the local culture in that particular area.

Their home church had been extremely irresponsible in its actions. They were not a missions agency, and they had no capabilities for training this missionary couple, let alone know what to do once the couple encountered problems. The end result was that this couple had become disillusioned. They questioned why this had happened to them and wondered if God even had a need for them in his kingdom. Our church, too, was partly to blame. We had supported them for the wrong reasons.

This experience also highlights the high attrition rate among the global sending missionary force. In 1994, the World Evangelical Fellowship Missions Commission launched the Reducing Missionary Attrition Project (ReMAP) to address specific issues related to long-term missionaries and undesirable attrition from active field service. The overall goal of the study was to reduce undesirable attrition in the long-term missionary body and thus increase the effectiveness of the global mission task force.

After two years of research and input from most of the global missions agency force, it was found that the attrition rate among both global and North American missionaries is one career missionary in twenty. That means that 5 percent of the missions force leaves the field to return home every year. At first, this doesn't seem like a very high number, but it is estimated that the current long-term, international, cross-cultural missionary force numbers about 150,000 (which is probably a very conservative number). An annual loss of 5 percent would be 7,500 missionaries leaving the field each year. Over a four-year term, this figure jumps to 30,000.

The study also found that the average agency loses 43 percent of its people over a ten-year period. They also found that the agencies with the lowest attrition rates had 50 percent more training requirements than those with higher attrition rates. So it's important to do your research.

There are also many different reasons for this attrition. Some attrition arises from things like normal retirement, issues related to children, a change in job description, or health issues, all of which would be considered acceptable attrition. Some attrition is preventable, even before a team leaves for the missions field. Preventable reasons for leaving the field include: lack of home support (not just financial), personal problems, lack of call, inadequate pre-field training, and inadequate commitment. Some attrition is the result of things that happen on the field, such as poor cultural adaptation and disagreement with the agency.

A third type of attrition would be desirable attrition. The first example, of the couple in Kenya that I shared on the previous pages would be an excellent example of desirable attrition that resulted from unrealized goals or results. Some people just aren't right for the missions field, no matter what setting they are placed in. The second example, with the couple in Mexico, would be an example of preventable attrition sadly turning to desirable attrition. There's nothing wrong with reducing the number of Western missionaries allowed to stay in the field; in fact, it could be healthy. But it requires courageous and proactive leadership from both the sending church and covering agency.

We have a responsibility to do the most with what God has given to us, and good intentions can't be the primary motivator of our reasoning and decision making. Jesus taught about this responsibility in Luke 12:48:

> *From everyone who has been given much, much will be demanded; and from the one who has been entrusted with much, much more will be asked.*

Global ministry teams have been entrusted with much, and we simply have to do a better job of bearing fruit with what we have been given.

This responsibility needs to be carried over to missions agencies, as well. There are many high-quality, result-driven agencies performing a vital role in kingdom work. Unfortunately, there are quite a few who are using outmoded paradigms and aren't producing much fruit. Some are still focused on countries that have long been reached for Christ. They continue to operate because well-meaning churches and individuals support them instead of challenging them to become more effective in areas that actually have a need.

As I stated in the beginning of this book, only 20 percent of all missions money goes to support foreign missions, while only .02 percent goes toward mission work among the un-evangelized. And we wonder why more of the world isn't being reached for Christ. We simply must do a better job. The best way we can glorify God is to "bear much fruit, showing yourselves to be my disciples." (John 15:8)

We must not be afraid to withdraw our support from poorly performing missions agencies. In fact, it's very biblical to do so. Jesus spoke to the Jews about this very subject in Matthew 21:43:

> *Therefore I tell you that the kingdom of God will be taken away from you and given to a people who will produce fruit.*

To do God's work should be viewed as a privilege, and one not to be taken lightly. Just look at the nation of Israel, which lost its privilege because of unfruitfulness.

I know this may sound harsh to some, but the reality is that if more church missions teams did their homework and focused their efforts and finances to support fruitful ministries that are reaching out in areas that have not yet heard the Gospel of Christ and end support for ineffective ministries, we would be making a lot more progress. The missions agencies that are under performing or working in areas already reached would be encouraged to change their focus and methods or discontinue their ministries.

A Case for Supporting National Church-Planters

It's been a year since David and Sandy Thanh came back from a trip to a country in Southeast Asia. Having lived in the United States since his family fled the area during the Vietnam War, this was his first chance to go back home and see his relatives after thirty years. David and Sandy have been Christians for many years, and while in Asia, he shares the Gospel with his relatives, and many come to Christ. Neither of them can escape the feeling that God wants to use them in a powerful way to reach out to the lost in David's former country.

David is a successful businessman, and Sandy has spent many years in the nursing field. He feels his business skills could be used to help farmers start their own local enterprises, and he could share the message of Christ in the process. Sandy feels she could use her skills doing outreach through local community health evangelism. But they have four children; two in grade school, one in junior high, and one in high school. They worry about how such a change might affect their children. They also worry about where their children will go to school.

Although David still speaks his native language fluently, it would take Sandy two years of extensive studies before she would be able to speak the native language. They realize that while many missionary couples homeschool their children, her need to do intensive language study the first two years would make this task next to impossible, and the children would have to go to a private, English-speaking school.

After many months of intensive prayer, family talks, and counsel with the leaders of their local home church, they decide on a plan to move to Southeast Asia. They go through all of the proper steps and channels, do extensive research on the region, and find coverage through a reputable missions agency. The Thanhs have definitely done their homework. Their ministry budget is then set and approved by their missions agency and, at the end of a year, they begin the process of visiting other local churches to raise support.

Their budget is by no means excessive compared to other Western missionaries, but raising support still presents a challenge for them. The agency decides that it would be best for David to work with a local Asian Christian Church in the capital city the first two years while Sandy learns the language. This will enable him to go through an orientation period and hopefully build a ministry team.

The Thanhs diligently send out financial and prayer support requests and share their ministry plans with any church willing to meet with them. The agency has stipulated that they cannot leave for Asia until they attain a support level of at least 75 percent of their budget. After nine months of fundraising, the Thanhs finally meet their minimum support goal and make plans to leave for Asia. It takes three more months to pack and make the final arrangements. Two years since they first made the decision to become missionaries, they finally arrive in Southeast Asia.

After unpacking and settling in the capital city, Sandy starts her language studies and David starts work with a local Christian church that is already engaged in local outreach and planting churches in nearby villages. Two years go by, and now Sandy has completed her studies and David has formed a ministry team with three other church workers.

They make the move to an unreached village in the northwest part of the country where David's former relatives live and begin to successfully reach out to local villagers by setting up low income loans, performing medical outreach, sharing the Gospel, baptizing new believers, and making Disciples of Christ.

One year later, after laying the groundwork for planting a church, the Thanhs head back to the United States for a one-year furlough, entrusting the ministry to their three fellow workers. While on furlough, a church plant is completed, with 140 regular attendees, half of whom have been baptized.

Six years after deciding to serve in Southeast Asia and after four years of financial support (three years in Asia plus one year of required furlough), a church has been planted for a cost of $232,600. This does not include the minimal cost of supporting the three members of their team, who are supported by the local church for that same four-year period.

The Thanh Family Ministry Budget			
Category		Sub-totals	Totals
1. Living Expenses (set by agency)			10800
2. Housing			4800
3. Routine Expenses			
Ministry travel		1500	
Holiday costs (including travel)		2500	
Other expenses		500	
	Total		4500
4. Other Current Expenses			
Annual Field Conference		500	
Language study and orientation		750	
Workshops and seminars		600	
	Total		1850
5. Savings and Ongoing Expenses			
Computer and IT equipment		250	
Vehicle purchase (amortized over 4 years)		875	
Moving and set up costs (set by agency)		3000	
Study and personal development		100	
Medical costs		2450	
Pension		7425	
	Total		14100

The Thanh Family Ministry Budget			
6. Children's Education	Total		9650
7. Shared Field Costs	Total		3250
8. Home Assignment Supplement	Total		9200
TOTAL FIELD COSTS Per Year		$	**58150**

Khem Chey is a man in his early thirties who lives in the same country the Thanhs have moved to. Recently married, he and his wife are expecting their first baby soon. Khem and his wife are farmers and work a small plot of land that his family has had for many generations. He lives in a small, one-bedroom home just like the rest of the people in his village. He is part of a continuous cycle of poverty, with little hope of ever breaking out of that cycle.

One day, a national Christian church planter comes to his village and shares the message of Christ with Khem. He encourages Khem to attend a Bible study in town where he can learn more about Jesus Christ. Intrigued, Khem accepts the invitation and, after a few weeks, accepts Christ. He is so excited about his Savior that he shares his new faith with his wife, and soon she also accepts Christ. For the next three months, Khem diligently attends the Bible study, and one day is rewarded with a gift of his own personal Bible.

The church planter can see that Khem possesses leadership gifts and asks him to start leading the Bible study. He tells Khem about a new two-year church planting class that will be starting soon and encourages him to enroll. The cost of the class is $2,000 and is more money than Khem has earned in his entire life. Khem would love to learn more about how to share his faith with others and wants to see his entire village come to Christ, but he has no money for school and is saddened at the potential lost opportunity to learn more about sharing his faith. He also worries about the loss of his income from not working his field and how he would support his wife and unborn child.

The church planter tells Khem that the agency he works with has sponsors from all over the world who all share his faith and might support him financially. He tells him the ministry agency will cover his tuition and family costs until a sponsor for him is found, and Khem enrolls in the class. Khem soon discovers that this is a hands-on class and in addition to his studies, is required to use the tools he learns to share his faith.

Khem learns how to communicate the Gospel naturally and appropriately for his culture. He invites people who are interested to come to his home where they study scripture, and he nurtures the newfound faith of those who decide to follow Christ. Three months go by, and Khem and his wife celebrate the birth of their baby. One week later, they get the good news that someone in the United States has sponsored his studies. While he is studying, Khem is given an allowance of one dollar per day—more than enough to meet his family's daily needs. In the meantime, Khem has already shared his faith with more than 120 people, and 50 of them have come to Christ.

After six months of study, Khem has shared the Gospel with another sixty people and led another thirty villagers into a relationship with Christ. He is now leading six Bible study groups with an average attendance of ten people. The people in the different small groups feel comfortable in a small group setting and openly encourage each other in their studies. Soon they are rewarded with their own Bible from the missions agency.

Khem starts the task of identifying members of his flock who possess leadership gifts. He selects three people to take over some of his small groups and disciple the growing group of believers. Khem submits the names of his three small group leaders to his ministry agency to be considered for a new church planting class starting at the beginning of the year, and they are accepted.

At the end of his first year of studies, Khem has led another sixty villagers to Christ and is now leading nine Bible study classes, with an average attendance of fifteen believers. He has learned how to form a membership class for new believers, which will eventually lead to a new church being established. After learning how to conduct baptismal services, half of the villagers in his Bible study classes have become baptized.

Soon, a new church is planted, and after eighteen months of studies, he now has twelve small groups under his care with an average attendance of fifteen people, and thirty more villagers become baptized. As his church grows, Khem teaches his members how to take responsibility for their own faith and share it with others. He also teaches them aspects of a healthy Christian marriage and tithing.

At the end of two years, Khem completes his studies. His church has grown to more than 250 regular attendees (half of whom have been baptized) and fifteen Bible study groups with an average attendance of fifteen people. He has to hold services in five different homes. The members of Khem's church now support him financially as their pastor, and the support he receives from the agency ends.

His three leaders have been enrolled in the church planting class for one year and have begun the church planting process with results almost identical to Khem's. They have already each identified three new group leaders who have been accepted for a church planting class starting the following year. A church planting movement has started.

The Chey Family Ministry Budget		Sub-totals	Totals
Category		**Sub-totals**	**Totals**
1. Living Expenses (including medical)			360
2. Housing			0
3. Routine Expenses			
Ministry travel (bicycle)		50	
	Total		410
4. Other Expenses			
Study Materials		190	
Church Planting Class Tuition		400	
	Total		590
TOTAL FIELD COSTS Per Year		$	**1000**

While the names of these two families are fictitious, their ministry examples are not. They are based on actual ministry partners I have been involved with in that region either personally or with missions teams I have been a part of. The church planting numbers are based on the average results I have seen in that particular country over the past six years. I used the example of three church planters in my example with Khem Chey because it tends to be the average in that particular region, and also to match the three team members with David Thanh.

Let's take a look not only at the side-by-side results of each ministry, but the growth over the first four-year ministry period.

	Western Missionary: The Thanhs	Native Church Planter: Khem Chey
End of Year One		
Gospel Shared	None	400
Conversions	None	140

	Western Missionary: The Thanhs	**Native Church Planter: Khem Chey**
In Study Groups	None	135
Baptisms	None	70
Churches Planted	None	None
New Church Planters	None	3
End of Year Two		
Gospel Shared	Minimal	1,800
Conversions	Few	960
In Study Groups	None	900
Baptisms	None	540
Churches Planted	None	1
New Church Planters	None	15
End of Year Three		
Gospel Shared	400	7,800
Conversions	140	3,060
In Study Groups	135	2,925
Baptisms	70	1,590
Churches Planted	None	4
New Church Planters	None	45
End of Year Four		
Gospel Shared	600	25,800
Conversions	240	9,360
In Study Groups	225	9,000
Baptisms	135	4,740
Churches Planted	1	19

	Western Missionary: The Thanhs	Native Church Planter: Khem Chey
New Church Planters	1	135

As you can see, there is quite a disparity between the results. We need to also look at the amount of time it took from the ministry's discovery and inception to the time the ministry actually started. The native church planter has a two-year head start, as he has none of the baggage of moving to an unfamiliar country. In fact, a native church planter has already planted a church by the time most Western missionaries get themselves moved and established.

The other consideration to think about is the exponential growth behind a native church planting movement. Let's add in the two years the Thanhs spent planning and raising support. The results are truly amazing.

	Western Missionary: The Thanhs	Native Church Planter: Khem Chey
End of Year One		
Gospel Shared	Planning	400
Conversions	Planning	140
In Study Groups	Planning	135
Baptisms	Planning	70
Churches Planted	Planning	None
New Church Planters	Planning	3
End of Year Two		
Gospel Shared	Fundraising	1,800
Conversions	Fundraising	960
In Study Groups	Fundraising	900
Baptisms	Fundraising	540
Churches Planted	Fundraising	1
New Church Planters	Fundraising	15

	Western Missionary: The Thanhs	**Native Church Planter: Khem Chey**
End of Year Three		
Gospel Shared	None	7,800
Conversions	None	3,060
In Study Groups	None	2,925
Baptisms	None	1,590
Churches Planted	None	4
New Church Planters	None	45
End of Year Four		
Gospel Shared	Minimal	25,800
Conversions	Few	9,360
In Study Groups	None	9,000
Baptisms	None	4,740
Churches Planted	None	19
New Church Planters	None	135
End of Year Five		
Gospel Shared	400	79,800
Conversions	140	28,260
In Study Groups	135	27,225
Baptisms	70	14,190
Churches Planted	None	64
New Church Planters	None	405
End of Year Six		
Gospel Shared	600	241,800
Conversions	240	84,960

	Western Missionary: The Thanhs	Native Church Planter: Khem Chey
In Study Groups	225	81,900
Baptisms	135	42,540
Churches Planted	1	199
New Church Planters	1	1,215

Besides the massive difference in results and costs, there is one other signifi-cant difference between these two types of ministries that highlights the funda-mental problem in missions today: with a Western, nonnative missionary, the focus is on the missionary instead of the mission. With all of the costs and per-sonal challenges a nonnative missionary faces just to plan, prepare, and adjust to a new environment, it can't be helped. But it also doesn't make it the best choice for your missions team.

The example I have used included a Western missionary couple that I know personally and think highly of. (Their names have been changed and the country they serve in was kept generic to maintain their privacy.) They are an example of a couple who has done everything they are supposed to do. This is a couple that by any standard would be a role model for Western missionaries. They were dili-gent in their research, had good training, got good support from their agency (which is well known and well respected), and have produced measurable results by Western missionary standards. That's what makes this example of a poten-tially outmoded paradigm all the more telling.

Even if all of the costs were the same, the results would still be heavily in favor of a national church planter. That is because people of a native country will almost always be more accepting of and open to someone of their own race, cul-ture, and color than they would regarding a Western missionary. They can relate to them, and there is a greater sense of trust. The only exception would be in a country or area where no native, national missionaries exist, and a true pioneer mission paradigm would need to be used.

Another problem is that we tend to reproduce who we are and what we know. If a missionary's main experience and background has been in a social, cultural, and economic system that produces large churches (i.e., North America), then it becomes much more difficult for that missionary to go to another part of the world or culture and succeed in establishing a church that is required to grow and thrive in the confines of a house or a garage.

Worse yet, my example used a Western missionary who actually spoke the native language (although his wife needed to learn), and he only needed an orientation period. Most Western missionaries need to spend at least one to two years immersed in language study to be able to fluently speak a new language before they can adequately share their faith and communicate in a different culture.

I haven't even mentioned the high attrition rate of first-time missionaries. According to the *Mission Handbook* published by MARC, 50 percent of all first-time missionaries struggle to adapt to their new surroundings and return stateside after only one term on the field. In the meantime, their higher funding support needs could have supported dozens of national church planting ministries for the same cost.

So you might be asking yourself, "With results this good, why hasn't the world been reached for Christ yet?" Because unfortunately, not enough individuals or churches (let's be honest—*especially churches*) support national church planters. Supporting a national church planter can be less personal. They don't come home for furlough. You can't bring them in front of your congregation unless their agency happens to bring them to the United States for a few weeks to build awareness of their ministries.

Sometimes it's hard to communicate with them because of language difficulties. In many cases, you can't communicate with them at all if they are in a politically sensitive country or part of a simplified church planting program under a regional director. But you can share their results. There's nothing that will excite congregations more than seeing or hearing the results of their investment in kingdom work. One just can't overlook the results that national church planters are attaining, especially compared with many Western missionaries.

Community Health Evangelism

In addition to sharing the Gospel, we have a responsibility to help those that are poor and needy in the world, and it should be an important aspect of every missions program. In fact, in Deuteronomy 15:11, God commands it:

> *Therefore I command you to be openhanded toward your brothers and toward the poor and needy in your land.*

The problem is that many concerned and caring missions teams end up funding programs that put a Band-Aid on poverty, providing temporary relief instead of funding solutions to the problem.

Too often, missions programs fund development strategies that rely on providing continuous financial support or sending in support packages and foreign experts to improve communities instead of teaching and empowering them to help themselves. Many times, this fosters dependence on the supporting church or foreign agency, which rarely results in lasting change. This type of program also can invite more corruption, which probably helped contribute to the poor condition in the first place.

The key is to equip and empower people to change themselves and their communities. This simple strategy is called Community Health Evangelism (CHE), and it can transform entire communities at a fraction of the cost of traditional development programs. This strategy was developed more than twenty years ago by Medical Ambassadors International (now LifeWind International) and has been adopted by many relief organizations and incorporated into the strategy of some missions agencies.

CHE is a strategy for finding long-term solutions to the real problems faced by the poor in the developing world. While there are some conditions that are prevalent in most communities, the CHE strategy is to find local leaders who can help identify the needs of their own particular community and then train and equip them to find solutions and initiate low-cost projects that will help improve those conditions.

The community projects might include simple things like teaching people how to prevent common diseases through health education, finding clean water sources, creating or improving agriculture, and teaching proper sanitation. In some projects, people are being taught to read or to establish their own very small businesses. The primary goal is to teach people how to do things for themselves. The key is finding good shepherds instead of just sheep.

By finding and training dedicated local leaders, the lives of entire communities can be enhanced because these leaders now demonstrate a spirit of love, cooperation, and mutual support. It also makes use of local assets, thereby reducing the need for outside funding. What's most impressive, though, is that CHE can evangelize an entire community, help people discover their self-worth, recover their dignity, and realize their full potential in God's kingdom.

It's all about community ownership. It teaches people in the community to take responsibility for everything that takes place in their village. CHE is a great multiplication strategy because the work expands as those who learn teach their neighbors what they have learned. It's also very sustainable, because the projects are locally led and in most cases free from dependence on outside resources.

Best of all, CHE is a wonderful strategy for planting churches and proclaiming the love of Jesus, not only in word but also in deed among the poor in developing countries. With every sharing of good deed is a sharing of God's word. This is because CHE training includes both physical and spiritual topics. Trained national workers who come to Christ bring people to Christ along with them. When people come to Christ, they are followed up, discipled, and organized into small groups. These groups then come together to form a church.

Another great thing about Community Health Evangelism is that it can be adapted for different situations. There are different CHE models that can be used in both open and restricted countries. Moral or ethical values are taught as part of the program, along with how to evangelize privately in one-on-one situations.

CHE expands a community's capacity to thrive because it touches every dimension of community life. It works because it stimulates people to use their full potential instead of treating them as helpless victims. It changes communities from the inside-out instead of the traditional outside-in missions strategy. Most importantly, it gives the local church that is created a leading role in building and improving their community, both physically and spiritually.

Through the use of CHE, people once helpless begin to have hope. Relationships are mended. Families learn how to properly care for their children. Entire communities learn to overcome their problems and begin to not only grow but thrive. That's because poverty can be overcome when people know Jesus Christ. They realize that God loves them too, for "precious is their blood in his sight." (Psalms 72:14)

We have an obligation to make our congregations aware of those less fortunate and to use the gifts we are blessed with to extend a helping hand. As Proverbs 14:21 says, "blessed is he who is kind to the needy."

National church planters and Community Health Evangelism are two great examples of modern missions paradigms that are taking place. The dynamics of the missions field are changing, and the Christian Church has a responsibility to respond properly. Paul taught in Ephesians 5:15–16:

> Be careful, then, how you live—not as unwise but as wise, making the most of every opportunity.

Missions teams need to continually investigate and stay updated on the latest changes in the missions field so that they can continually improve and "make the most of every opportunity."

CHAPTER 5

▼

MINISTRY PARTNERSHIPS
AND PROJECTS

Building relationships with agencies and ministry partners and investing in projects usually accounts for the bulk of funding money raised in a missions program. Yet this is where many teams do the worst job when it comes to good stewardship habits. They employ a technique I call "paint-by-numbers ministry." They stumble along with no real plan or guidelines for reviewing proposals, adding ministry partners, or reviewing their performance in the field.

Proposals for projects and ministry partners are reviewed and approved as they come in, without ever discerning if the proposals match up well with their church or understanding if the projects are actually cost effective or not. When an existing partner is either struggling, or underperforming, we excuse them because their heart is in the right place, and we don't hold them accountable. This type of attitude needs to change. It's not healthy for either the church or the ministry partners, and it certainly doesn't satisfy God's goals of expanding his family.

Before a potential ministry partner even submits a support proposal, I would recommend that you have them fill out a questionnaire created by your missions team. This serves two different purposes. One, it helps you evaluate the potential partner, assess their skills and capabilities, and also evaluate their compatibility with the direction of your team. Second, it actually helps the potential ministry partner think through and evaluate different aspects of their ministry.

There are standard questions that should be asked by every missions team, and some of these would also be replicated on the ministry review form covered later in this book:

1. Are you a first-time missionary or are you currently active in ministry?

2. If active, how many years have you been in the field?

3. What is the primary focus of your ministry?

4. What are you most passionate about in missions work and why? (If new to the missions field, please skip to question 15)

5. Please briefly state your ministry accomplishments this past twelve months, identifying how your ministry has changed the lives of the people you are serving.

6. How many people have you or any member of your ministry led to Christ in the last twelve months?

7. What kind of follow-up and discipleship are you doing with them?

8. Are you personally training an apprentice or any church planters at this time? If yes, please describe.

9. How much of your time is spent with the local people/target group?

10. How many local churches/missions groups are you impacting or working with?

11. How many churches have been planted in the past four years from your ministry? (Please describe)

12. If you are a teacher at a Bible college or a field trainer: How many students went out and planted new churches?

13. What were your goals for this past year and were they realized? (Please give examples of both realized and un-realized goals if any.)

14. Have you hosted any short-term teams before? If so, what was the purpose of their visit?

15. What is your ministry plan for the coming year? (If you are on furlough, what are your plans for your furlough and for your first year when you return to the field?)

16. What is your exit strategy for this particular ministry and location?

17. How will you define success?

18. How active is your agency in supporting your ministry, and how often does someone from the agency visit you on the field?

19. If you could do anything you wanted in your field and resources were no object, what would it be?

20. a. What is your current personal support (normal living costs, retirement, health insurance, etc.) level budget? Budget $ _____/month vs. Actual $_____/month

   b. What is your current ministry support level per month? Budget $_____/month vs. Actual $_____ (Please specify what these funds are being used for.)

Additional Questions for First-Time Missionaries:

1. Please describe your previous ministry involvement and experience.

2. Will you be involved primarily in church planting, training or both?

3. What made you select the country or people group you are planning to serve in?

4. Have you been to this country?

5. Are there any Christian churches planted in this area? Questions six and seven are the two most important questions you can ask a new missionary:

6. Are any other missionaries, trainers or agencies supporting national church planters currently working in this particular country, location or with this particular people group?

7. If so, what do you believe you will be able to do that would be different from them, make you more successful and not duplicate their efforts?

8. Are you fluent in the native language? If not, how long will it take you to learn it?

9. How many churches are currently supporting you?

10. How many individuals are currently supporting you?

Having a questionnaire for prospective ministry partners lets them know you are serious about the stewardship of your congregation's missions money and the support you might provide the missionary. It also lets them know that you will hold them accountable for their performance on the missions field. In the case of a first-time missionary about to leave home, it forces them to evaluate aspects of their potential ministry and personal gifting that they may not have thought about before. This can be a very healthy thing for them to do.

One of the keys to making good decisions is to have guidelines that not only allow for proper assessment of proposals, but provide clear guidelines of expectations and responsibilities for the potential partner or agency. After all, "If you search for good you will find favor." (Prov. 11:27; NLT)

Assessing Potential Ministry Partners

Every missions team has areas of ministry that are more important to them than others, or have a higher priority in outreach based on the makeup of the team or the congregation. For some churches, this might mean supporting and being involved with ministries that have an emphasis on helping children or community development. For others, it might mean community health evangelism or medical outreach. For some, it might be Bible translation or supply. All areas are needed and useful; it comes down to a matter of interest for the team and church.

It's important to create a set of values that give you the ability to properly weigh a proposal and give it an overall score. The more important the aspect of ministry, the higher a potential score should be assigned to that area. This creates a weighted score sheet, or what I like to call a missions matrix. You should have a separate one for evaluating potential ministry partners and one for one-time project proposals. Each should have a separate set of criteria that is weighted accordingly.

The great thing about a missions matrix is that it can be also used to evaluate a currently supported ministry partner on a yearly basis. It also gives you a good supporting document to send with a proposal recommendation to a church leadership or elder board. It shows the team has done their homework and has a healthy, unbiased process in place for evaluation. Each team member should apply this matrix personally to the proposal. Then, at a team meeting, everyone shares their scores for each of the attributes, one attribute at a time. A consensus should be reached for each attribute and ultimately a final total and score. The higher the score, the higher the chance the project might be funded.

For a missionary matrix, the values need to include a score for the ministry target area, the type of ministry, the essentiality of the ministry, the missionary's field experience, the capability of the missionary and his or her appropriate gifting, any problems or distractions that might hinder the missionary, and the quality of the mission agency's coverage. The two highest or most important weightings should be the ministry target area and the type of ministry. Below is a sample of a matrix complete with an explanation for the thinking behind each section.

MMC Global Ministry Team
Missionary Matrix

Missionary: _____ **Agency:** _____

Ministry Target

20—Unreached National

18—Unreached Nonnative Trainer

16—Unreached Nonnative_____

14—Reached Limited Exposure—National

12—Reached Limited Exposure—Nonnative Trainer

10—Reached Limited Exposure—Nonnative_____

8—Reached Frequent Exposure—Specific Target Area

6—Unreached Administration (works on behalf of)

4—Reached Limited Exposure Administration (works on behalf of)

2—Local Ministry **Ministry Target Score (____)**

This section is based on modern missions paradigms that show (in general) that properly trained nationals are doing a more effective job of outreach and evangelization than Western missionaries for the same amount of money. A ministry to or in an unreached area should always be given a higher priority and score than a reached area, but consideration should be given to a "hot spot" where the Holy Spirit's work is attracting special focus. The definition of an administration position assumes they are someone working in the States on behalf of a reached or unreached country. Finally, local ministry is someone who is reaching out to a specific culture in a local U.S. community setting.

Type of Ministry

20—Church Planting Evangelism and Discipleship

18—Leadership Training

16—Community Development

14—Medical or Relief Work

12—Foreign Based Support Services

10—Linguistics and Translation

8—Field Administration

6—USA-Based—Evangelism

4—USA-Based—Support Services

2—USA-Based—Administration **Ministry Type Score (____)**

This section is pretty self-explanatory and provides for flexibility in the weighting process based on your church or team's priorities or interests. It is just an example. It does not suggest that someone involved in church planting is better or more important than someone involved in linguistics. If your team values, let's say, medical relief work as a high priority over other types of ministry, then there would be nothing wrong with assigning it a score of 20 instead of 14. This weighting does assume that U.S.-based "missionaries" have less of a direct impact on global missions than do foreign-based ministry partners.

Essentiality of Ministry

6—Strategic and Necessary

4—Useful

2—Could Be Done by Others **Essentiality Score (____)**

You have to ask the question, is the type of ministry this potential ministry partner involved in strategic in nature? Is it necessary for a breakthrough in sharing the Gospel in a particular area? If so, score it high; if it's useful among many other options, perhaps a little lower. If it is something that can be done by others, you have to decide if their ministry is actually needed. Perhaps they do it better than others.

Capability of Missionary and Appropriate Gifting

5—Effective, Successful

3—Above Average

1—Average **Capability Score (_____)**

This is mostly self-explanatory. If a potential ministry partner is just preparing to go out into the field, you have to give them a score of zero in this category.

Missionary Experience

3—Significant Ministry Experience

2—Moderate Ministry Experience

1—Minimal Ministry Experience **Experience Score (_____)**

I usually suggest basing these scores on significant experience being more than ten years, moderate as five to ten years, and minimal as less than three years. Some churches use a five years or more, three years or less, or one year or less ratio to score this section. You will notice that the score weighting is lower for this category than the Capability or Gifting of a missionary section above because this section is more a matter of tenure than effectiveness.

Personal Problems and Distractions

3—No or Few Distractions

2—Relatively Free from Problems

1—Somewhat Incapacitated **Personal Score (_____)**

Language barriers, family issues, support shortfalls, and health issues all can play a role in complicating ministry efforts. You can't avoid asking some personal questions here. Do they know the language? If not, how long would it take them to learn it? Also ask for a copy of their ministry budget. Has their agency approved it? Does it seem excessively high to you? If so, it could be a sign of extra health care needs, school tuition for kids, or other things. Ask yourself, could someone else do this for less money?

Quality of Missions Agency

3—High

2—Above Average

1—Average **Agency Score (____)**

How solid is the missions agency? What kind of oversight and leadership does it provide to the missionary? How frequently does a representative perform field visits? How long has the agency been around? What are their success stories? How much of their budget goes towards overhead? (5% or less is great, 10% is average, and any agency over 15% you should start questioning.)

Highest Total Rating Score Available = 60 Actual Score (____)
Percentage Score (____)

Divide the actual score by the total rating score available to get a percentage score. A numerical score of 47 would become a percentage score of 78 percent. Once you have a percentage score, your team needs to decide what the minimum score threshold should be in order for a ministry or project to be recommended to your elder board. My recommendation is that a proposal should have a score of at least 70 percent in order to be sent to leadership.

Assessing Potential Ministry Projects

The matrix below should be used to filter mission's project proposals. The categories and weightings are slightly different because there is more emphasis on the project and the ministry agency and less on a particular person or people. It is divided into three distinct sections: scope, need, and relationship. With a ministry partner relationship, your view should be long-term; with a project, it should be on immediate impact and strategy.

MMC Global Ministry Team
Ministry Project Matrix

Primary Target People

5—Unreached

3—Least Evangelized

1—Reached Christians **Target People Score (____)**

This section should be approached the same as the ministry partner rubric.

Primary Target Place

5—Third World

3—Second World

1—First World (USA and Canada = 0) **Target Place Score (____)**

According to most encyclopedias, the First World consists of the developed nations of the United States, Canada, Western Europe, Japan, Singapore, Taiwan, Australia, and New Zealand. The Second World consists of the developing nations in Eastern Europe, the former Soviet states, China, India, South Korea, South Africa, the Middle East, Mexico, Costa Rica, Panama, Philippines, South Korea, and most of the Caribbean. Third World countries tend to be desperately poor; they might have one or two modern cities, but the rest of the country is in extreme poverty. These countries would include most of Africa, Southeast Asia, Central America, Pakistan, Afghanistan, and Indonesia. The key here is to ask where in a particular country the ministry is taking place. If you went to Vietnam and the ministry was in Ho Chi Minh City, it would be Second World. But head into the highlands or vast Mekong River Delta areas, and you are now Third World.

Potential Gospel Reach

5—100,000 people

4—50,000 people

3—10,000 people

2—1,000 people

1—100 people **Gospel Reach Score (____)**

What is the potential number of people to be reached as a direct result of this project?

Ministry Domain

5—Church Plant

3—Evangelize or Relief Work

1—Disciple and Develop

0—Administrative **Domain Score (_____)**

This section should be approached the same as the ministry partner matrix.

Ministry Activity

5—Equip and Train

3—Planning and Development

1—Logistics and Support

0—Maintenance **Activity Score (_____)**

This section should be approached the same as the ministry partner matrix.

Essentiality

6—Significant and Necessary

4—Useful

2—Emergency **Essentiality Score (_____)**

This section should be approached the same as the ministry partner matrix.

Impact and Longevity

3—Catalyst

2—Less than two years

1—More than two years

0—Perpetual **Impact Score** (___)

With projects, it's important to see more immediate results. That's because by their very nature, projects can provide a real turning point for a ministry. Sometimes a specific outreach or event can be the catalyst for making inroads in an area that was a struggle before. I assign a higher score to projects that have a specific purpose and a specific outcome, rather than projects that last a long time or are perpetual by nature, such as supporting an ongoing feeding program. If a project lasts more than three months, you should consider adding the ministry that oversees it as a monthly ministry partner. An exception would be funding the building of a school or ministry building, or perhaps a series of community outreach events.

Leverage or Strategy

3—Very High

2—High

1—Moderate

0—Low **Leverage Score** (___)

Every ministry project has its own unique purpose, and you have to look at the proposal and grade it by how well it applies to the area of ministry. Is the project really going to make a difference for that ministry or that area?

Association with MMC

3—More than five years

2—Three to five years

1—Less than three years (none = 0) **Association Score** (___)

The longer or stronger relationship with the missions agency or ministry partner, the higher the score.

Agency Track Record

3—Exceeds Expectations

2—Meets Expectations

1—Limitations **Agency Score (____)**

Does the agency or ministry have a history of being successful and completing their projects? Do the projects consistently come in under budget? Have previous projects really changed lives or helped the ministry? Are there conditions unique to the area that might limit the effectiveness or the project or outreach? What is the ministry agency's yearly overhead cost?

Accountability Structure

3—Exceeds Expectations

2—Meets Expectations

1—Limitations **Accountability Score (____)**

Who is ultimately responsible for the project's success? What is the person or agency going to do to help insure completion?

Potential for Feedback

3—MMC Point Person

2—Missionary

1—Agency Only (No contact = 0) **Feedback Score (____)**

Is the project going to be directly monitored by a member of your team or another church member? Or are you going to be kept informed of progress by a supported missionary or agency official?

Highest Total Rating Score Available = 50 Actual Score (____)
Percentage Score (____)

These two matrix examples are just that—examples. Every ministry team has slightly different values and priorities. The key is to set up a scoring system for your proposals that emphasizes those values and weights them accordingly. If over time your team changes some of its priorities, make sure and change the scoring system appropriately. Ultimately, a matrix is a valuable tool that takes subjectivity out of proposal decision making. Each proposal has to stand on its own merit, and this is a healthy process for helping them do so.

Sending Proposals to Your Elder Board

This is perhaps one of the most overlooked tasks that global ministry leaders need to perform well. Some of you will read this, roll your eyes, and say, "I can't believe he's covering something so basic." That's because you are looking at it from a "basic" point of view. Most ministry leaders send proposal recommendations to their elder boards with very little information and an air of expectation that their proposals should basically be rubber-stamped by church leadership. After all, if you've done your homework and thoroughly researched a proposal, why should the team be second-guessed?

This is somewhat of an arrogant approach to take (even if it's unintentional), and you miss out on a chance to not only educate the church leadership but also raise their interest and gain their valuable support. Proposals should always be sent with a humble heart, which is pleasing to God. 1 Peter 5:5 says:

> *Young men [and women], in the same way be submissive to those who are older. Clothe yourselves with humility toward one another because, God opposes the proud but gives grace to the humble.*

I have seen many proposals that are sent as line-item proposals or are combined into brief summary sheets with very little information provided to substantiate the proposal. To illustrate my point, I have a copy of a proposal that was sent to an elder board at a church I spent some time with:

Proposal for the Pastor/Elder Meeting

Proposal: To support nationals involved with the Africa Mission Agency—church planters [The words "church planters" were handwritten]

Reason: Amy Henderson and Sandy Irving will be attending the next Africa Mission Conference in Africa, where they will be spending four days meeting the nationals and attending their meetings. They will have an excellent opportunity to meet possible nationals whom MMC could consider "family." Since Amy and Sandy will be there, they can take their pictures and get their biographies, so we're not supporting someone "out there," but people about whom we have some knowledge.

Idea: Through prayer, these two ladies would be sensitive to the Holy Spirit's guidance to find up to 10 (or more?) nationals for $50 monthly [the next section is blacked out with felt pen]. They will contact Ramon to indicate their interest before leaving.

Wow, what a missed opportunity due to so much missing information. The first problem is that there is no team decision indicated here. It sounds as if the decision would be made at the whim of these two ladies, not on a recommendation from the team. The words "church planters" were handwritten and added as an afterthought in case the elder board didn't know who nationals were. The way the word "nationals" is used sounds so derogatory that one might as well say "natives." Where is the budget in all of this? How is the board supposed to approve something with no firm numbers? It gives the appearance that the team expects a blank check, or at the very least an open pocketbook.

There is no information on the accomplishments of the agency or what their track record is in the missions field. What is the relationship of the agency with the church? How did the proposal come about? Was it initiated by the team or the agency? How many missionaries does the agency have? How many church planters have they trained? What are the average results of this agency's church planters? How do they perform their ministry? How long will they need to be supported? Does the agency have an exit strategy? How do they define success? For that matter, how would the team? By the way, who is Ramon?

You don't need to provide every little detail behind your team's decision, but you do need to give your elder board a reason to support your recommendation. You should also explain how a particular proposal ties into or supports your ministry team's overall strategy. More importantly, every proposal recommendation is an opportunity to not only gain support for your proposal but for your ministry, as well. The more you help them know, the more their support and respect for the team will grow.

Guidelines for Ministry Partners and Accountability

Once you have approved a new ministry partner, it's important to give them guidelines and share your expectations for the partnership. I always feel it's a privilege to participate in the blessings of a ministry and look forward to a fruitful partnership. In order for your team to serve them and to respond to their ministry needs, you need to have timely communication and a willingness (and openness) on their part to share information with you. The guidelines you create should include the responsibilities of the ministry partner and the responsibilities of your team. There should also be a clear exit strategy, should you ever feel the need to take it.

Ministry partners who receive regular support from your church should agree to full disclosure of all sources of income and funding partners. Having a policy of full disclosure allows you and your team the opportunity to monitor your ministry partner's total support income. It is always helpful to know who else is supporting them, so that if funding support starts to drop, you can contact other supporters and find out if they have the same concerns you do.

Be clear about your expectations from all ministry partners. If you want them to provide timely ministry updates, prayer requests, and photos, be specific and state how often. I would recommend at least quarterly updates and monthly prayer requests if possible. Ask them if you can share non personal information with your congregation, unless its otherwise specified as sensitive in nature, so that the church body has a chance to learn about the ministry, be involved in prayer support, and share in the blessings of the ministry.

All of your ministry partners should be expected to make themselves available to meet with the team and speak in front of the congregation when visiting in the United States or on furlough. Nothing can replace direct contact between a ministry partner and the congregation. In addition to giving them a chance to share their ministry to the church body as a whole, try to set aside an area where church members can meet and speak with missionaries before and after services.

Many churches only review ministry partners when they visit or come home for furlough every three years. I believe that all ministry partners should be reviewed annually to help you determine if their needs are being met and to evaluate if their ministry work is productive and fruitful. This is not only prudent, it's biblical: "Thus, by their fruit you will recognize them." (Matt. 7:20)

If this is your team's policy, let your new ministry partners know this when they sign on. Include it in your guidelines and send out an annual review form at least ninety days before your fiscal year end. Give them time to respond, but state a deadline for their being completed and returned to the team. With e-mail, there really isn't any reason why your ministry partners can't respond in a timely manner.

Remember that your ministry partner is busy working in the field, so keep your annual review form simple and to the point. It should contain questions that help guide them toward giving your team an idea of the current status of their ministry, including highlights and any problems that might potentially impact their ministry. You also want to find out what their goals and plans are for the following years so you have a measuring tool for their next review. Below is a sample of a simple Ministry Partner Annual Review Form.

Missions Minded Church
Ministry Partner Annual Review

Dear MMC Ministry Partner: The following questions are provided to help guide you toward giving us an idea of the current status of your ministry, including the highlights and any problems that might potentially impact your ministry. All answers will be kept confidential within the Global Ministry Team.

1. Please briefly state your ministry accomplishments over the past twelve months, and identify how your ministry has changed the lives of the people you are serving.

2. a. Have you personally or has any member of your ministry led any people to Christ in the last 12 months? If so, how many people? What kind of follow-up and discipleship are you doing with them?

    b. Approximately, how many people have you had the opportunity to personally share Christ with in the past 12 months?

    c. Are you personally discipling anyone or training an apprentice at this time? If yes, describe.

    d. How much of your time is spent with the local people/target group?

    e. How many local churches/missions groups are you impacting or working with?

3. Are you anticipating any changes in your ministry this coming year, such as change in location, agency or specific area of ministry? If yes, please detail.

4. a. What do you see as possible obstacles that you, your team or your strategy face for the following year?

    b. Are you currently experiencing any conflicts with other missionaries or your agency?

    c. Is your agency supporting you and responsive to your needs?

d. Is there anything we as a church can do that your agency is not doing?

5. a. What is your current personal support (normal living costs, retirement, health insurance etc.) level budget? Budget $ _____/month vs. Actual $_____/month

    b. What is your current ministry support level per month? Budget $_____/month vs. Actual $_____ (Please specify what these funds are being used for.)

6. Do you have a spiritual and emotional accountability partner that can speak truth into your life and ministry?

7. Please comment on your prayer and devotional life. (Tell us what you are reading that encourages you and challenges you and if you are journaling your thoughts and prayers.)

8. Is there anything we at MMC could be doing to better support your ministry?

9. Please share with us a brief overall vision of your ministry plan for next year:

Missions Team Responsibilities

Inform any new ministry partners as soon as you begin full monthly support, after elder board approval. If you have ministry promotional vehicles such as bookmarks, bulletin inserts, or a Web site, let your new ministry partners know. Ask them to provide you with a personal bio that includes background information on themselves and their ministry, as well as general prayer requests. The team should make it their obligation to share prayer requests (unless sensitive in nature) and highlight the ministry goals and accomplishments of every ministry partner with the congregation.

When your ministry partners are visiting or are on furlough, your team should make every effort to provide housing or a place to stay and help with transportation during visits to your church. Let them know you will make every effort to create opportunities for them to share with the congregation. It should go without saying that your team pray regularly for the needs of all of your ministry partners.

Occasionally, ministry partners have to change direction or are reassigned to a different area or a new type of ministry. If you and your team come to the conclusion that it is time to discontinue financial support for a ministry partner, it should come as no surprise to your partner. They should know you have concerns early on, and they should know at the time you start support what possible reasons might lead to termination of funding support. I would recommend an immediate review and possibly terminating funding support for the following reasons:

1.) The affiliation of the missionary with his or her board or agency has been changed or severed.

2.) A substantial moral problem arises.

3.) There is a determination of unsatisfactory performance by the committee after review of the ministry.

4.) The ministry partner demonstrates a lack of financial accountability or poor financial stewardship.

5.) Adequate evaluation of the missionary's ministry is not provided, or there is a lack of returned annual review.

6.) Consistent lack of availability by ministry partner when in-country or on furlough.

7.) A personal problem arises that requires the ministry partner to leave or change their field of service.

8.) The ministry partner fails to correspond with your team on a minimum quarterly basis.

9.) The missionary relocates for personal reasons, or takes a ministry position in the U. S.

10.) The ministry partner's assignment (field of service) changes.

11.) The ministry partner's biblical or theological doctrine is no longer in alignment with your church.

12.) The missionary's ministry no longer matches the overall focus and direction of your missions program or your church.

You should have a clearly defined policy or procedure for dropping support for a ministry partner, complete with timelines. It should be simple and to the point, yet the process should honor the missionary and give them a chance to respond to your concerns or decision. The guidelines below will give you an idea of timelines and procedures.

Severing Ministry Partner Relationships

I usually recommend that all ministry partners be sent out a ministry review form ninety days prior to the end of their individual twelve-month support period. These should be sent out every year, on time, without hesitation or delay. The ministry partner should be made aware in a separate cover letter that they have thirty days from the date they receive the questionnaire to complete and return the form to you so your team has adequate time to evaluate their ministries. Should your ministry team find in favor of recommending termination of a partnership, that recommendation should be then forwarded to the elder board for approval along with the specific reasons for termination of support.

If the recommendation for termination is approved by your elder board, you should then send a letter of intended termination to the ministry partner, complete with an outline of concerns or reasons for termination. The letter should encourage the ministry partner to respond within thirty days to your concerns in order to allow your team adequate time to evaluate the missionary's response. If the ministry partner happens to be in-country, then your team should set time aside to meet with the missionary face-to-face.

Your team should then make every effort to meet with or review the response from the ministry partner within thirty days and forward the final termination recommendation, with specific reasons cited, to the elder board for final approval. Your team should operate with a sense of respect, but also with a sense of urgency. If your ministry partner has taken the time to meet your deadlines, then your team needs to respond in the same manner, even if it means calling a special team meeting.

I would recommend that the original termination letter should inform the ministry partner that their funding will continue an additional ninety days from their individual fiscal year end (as severance) at full support to allow them time to raise support from other sources for funding or adjust their budgets accordingly. At the end of the ninety-day grace period, the ministry partnership should be officially terminated.

Sometimes you need to initiate the drop process with a ministry partner to get their attention (although that's usually a warning sign that the missionary isn't doing a very good job in the first place). It is imperative that you follow through with a drop process when one has been initiated. It is one thing if a ministry partner addresses your concerns to the point where you decide to continue support, but it's another if they can't (or don't), and you still elect to continue supporting them.

Some teams are afraid of hurting someone's feelings; others are just too lazy to go through with it and choose to ignore all of the obvious facts for making the decision. They opt instead to continue to support poor performance or a change in ministry direction that is in not in alignment with the team. At that point, it just shows poor judgment and makes a mockery of your ministry, which is not honoring of God. Proverbs 3:21 makes it very clear that we should "preserve sound judgment and discernment, do not let them out of your sight."

I have seen members of missions teams try to justify their lack of a decision by saying things like, "They're going through a tough time right now, and we shouldn't add to it," or, "He or she means well," or my all-time favorite, "It's tough out there on the field." Instead of allowing God to challenge them, we go out of our way to shelter them. In the process, we have confused the idea of being a source of comfort to them with being a source of strategic support for them. We are in essence helping them feel more "comfortable" with life.

Sometimes, in order to achieve success, we have to do a little trimming. We have to "test everything and hold on to the good." (1 Thess. 5:20) Sometimes the biggest favor we can do for someone is too "allow" them to be trimmed, for then they have an opportunity to take stock of their situation, face the issues that trouble them or are holding them back, and make the changes that are needed so they might grow and bear fruit. We can't (and shouldn't) protect and shelter them from God's clippers. For as we enable their issues to grow through avoidance, it will take larger shears to prune, and the cuts will be even more painful in the future.

If you have screened your ministry partners well at the front end, supported them with constant prayer, and monitored their progress over the seasons, you shouldn't have reason to terminate many partnerships. But things can change over time, and if there comes a point where the team realizes it has to make a change, it should feel comfortable doing so. You have to not only honor your ministry partners but also the process. Your ministry partners will respect you for it, and the members of your church who trust you with their money will as well.

CHAPTER 6

▼

MINISTRY STRATEGY AND PLANNING

Most people, whether Christian or not, tend to support or participate in a cause if what they see or hear is compelling to them. It has to resonate with their inner feelings in a way that stirs their hearts and then their minds to take action. The world of missions isn't any different. It must be presented in a way that provides a sense of not only need, but also urgency. Missions must also be presented in a way that reminds fellow Christians of their obligation to share the message of Christ in their neighborhood and in other parts of the world.

The challenge we face is with Christians who are nominal or institutional Christians at best. Every church has them, and there are probably more that exist than most church leaders would be willing to admit. These Christians are more inwardly motivated, with more concern about the color of the sanctuary carpets, the comfort of the pews, the programs available for them and their children, or what the worship music should sound like on Sundays. To reach these types of Christians, you have to have a strategy that will motivate them to want to get involved. Your job is to make missions so exciting that they feel like they are missing out when they don't participate.

There are four key components that should be incorporated into a successful missions program strategy: increasing awareness, increasing participation, increasing support, and celebrating results. Each of these is equally important, and none of them should be overlooked. At the beginning of each fiscal year, the team should get together and look for new ways to address all of the components.

Increasing Awareness

This strategy component is all about sharing the vision of the team and the program, and the emphasis here is on creating communication vehicles to the congregation. The way you present missions to the rest of the congregation goes a long way in determining how successful your missions program will be. You have to be able to inform them and at the same time grab their attention, make them think, and stimulate their curiosity to know more. This may seem deliberate to some people; I'd prefer to think of it as strategic.

Church Missions Web Site Content

Since most communication vehicles involve competing either for time on the pulpit or space in the church bulletin, utilizing the space on your church Web site is a great place to build visibility to promote missions. In fact, it should be at the very heart of all your communications. Every communication you have with the congregation, either verbal or in print, should refer church members back to the Web site for more information. The global ministry section of your church Web site needs to stimulate the reader both visually and verbally and encourage them to visit every page. When you design and build your global ministry Web pages, they should include:

1. A general home page describing the purpose of your global ministry team—why it exists and how it operates.

2. Individual "Meet our Missionaries" pages for each ministry partner, complete with ministry details, personal and ministry photos, country flag and map, e-mail contact info, general prayer requests, and the strategic nature of your ministry partnership as a church. Consider adding a section of fun facts for every ministry partner country. Remember the key here is to give the average church member as many ways as possible to help stimulate their memory for the missions program. If the picture of a flag or an interesting fact help will help them remember you have a missionary in Cambodia that needs their prayer or financial support, then you need to include it.

3. A financial page complete with the missions budget breakdown and a colorful graph or pie chart. People want to know where their money is going and how it's being used. If you run on a faith promise program, show a

year-to-date budget comparison that's updated weekly or at least monthly. (Hopefully this information is provided in your church bulletin each week also.) Graphs or pie charts are important because many people respond better to visuals than words.

4. A monthly updated praise report (ministry partner news) and prayer request page. Nothing draws interest more than when you share success stories from your ministry partners as well as their prayer requests. It gives the congregation an opportunity to partner in prayer and learn first-hand of the challenges on the missions field.

5. A running yearly highlight summary page (See "Celebrate Results").

6. A "How you can help" page featuring different ways congregation members can become involved with missions.

7. A "Calendar of events" page for scheduled short-term trips, missions functions, and home missionary visits.

8. A page with links for all of the ministry agencies your team partners with and links to missions informational Web sites. (See my Web site for examples.)

9. A page with recommended missions books, including photos of book covers and possible short reviews or descriptions of each book.

Bookmarks and Bulletin Inserts

Many churches have very tight controls on what can be inserted into the weekly bulletin. If your church leadership will approve it, try to find a permanent space in the weekly bulletin for missions news, ministry partner updates, and prayer requests. If you can't get that approved, there are a couple of other approaches you might take. A two-sided "Missionary of the Month" bookmark can break down the barrier to inserts by allowing the church to utilize one side of the bookmark to list upcoming events, post a monthly Bible reading guide, or any other vehicle of the church's choosing.

The best bookmarks have the missionary's name, an abbreviated ministry description, photo, country flag, e-mail contact info, and of course your church Web site on one side and the church logo and content on the other, all printed on a graphic background (field of flowers, mountain scene, etc). The bookmark should be included at the same time every month so members get used to seeing it on a regular basis. If a bookmark looks good, people will use it. Make sure to have extras available in your missions resource area, with occasional bookmark awareness announcements.

Create a missions "Praise Report" bulletin insert with current ministry partner news from each of your ministry partners on one side and their prayer requests on the other side. Try to get one included in your bulletin at least quarterly, and if you succeed in getting inserted monthly, make sure and stagger it with the inclusion of bookmark. This insert should be duplicated on your Web site. Of course, always include the missions pages of your church Web site on the insert for more information.

Other Awareness Vehicles

Create "Missionary of the Month" posters for all of your ministry partners to correspond with the monthly bookmark and have them displayed on poster stands in your lobby or entryway. The posters should contain a picture of the missionary (or family), country flag, location of missionary country, affiliated missions agency, and your missions team tagline, such as "Committed to Reaching the World.".

Work with your teaching pastor staff to schedule visiting ministry partners to share a story or some ministry highlights for three to five minutes between worship time and the sermon on Sunday mornings. Include them in your Sunday service prayers. You could also announce that the missionary would be available in a specific area after service to answer any questions, then encouraging people to introduce themselves to the missionaries.

Create a missions magnet with your missions team slogan over a picture of a needy child, someone receiving Christ, receiving a Bible, etc., and add your church or team logo to it to serve as a reminder of the Great Commission. And yes, place the Web site on it.

The advancement in technology opens up other potential opportunities to promote missions, should your budget allow for it. Consider adding a missions blog on your church Web site and invite members and ministry partners to interact with each other. You could bring in a live video feed from your ministry partners on the field and allow them to talk directly to the congregation during a Sunday service.

Building awareness also requires educating the congregation about God's calling in our lives for missions and the Great Commission. You should challenge your team to create and offer simplified missions classes or short courses. You could call them "Becoming a World Christian" classes or something like that. At the first church I attended, they offered a six-week mini-perspectives course entitled "Vision for the Nations." Our missions pastor taught one of the classes and lined up guest speakers or other team members to teach the rest. It was more interesting because we had a different speaker each week. These classes should actually be a part of a much larger foundational class program, but more on that later.

Every church with a missions program should hold a yearly missions festival or at the very least a "missions awareness week." While your goal should be to create as many opportunities to share missions throughout the year as possible, you should always create a special time for the entire church to inspire people to the call and celebrate what God is doing in the world.

At my last church we had two missions awareness weeks—one to kick off our faith promise campaign, and another six months later to help refocus our congregation and give them a public update on what we were doing and what had been accomplished. There should also be an active strategy to increase the amount of missions-related Sunday announcements per year.

This is at the very least a bare minimum of what your team should attempt to do in order to increase awareness of your missions program and your ministry partners. The most important thing is to be creative and never forget that how you present something is almost as important as what you present.

Increasing Participation

This strategy component is centered on creating opportunities to get the congregation more involved in missions activities. The key is to not only help individuals get involved, but the congregation as a whole. The more you can get people to work together for a specific mission's cause, the better. It's imperative that your missions team lead the congregation in developing a strategic focus for the congregation's involvement in urban and global evangelization. We have a biblical responsibility to help people "put into practice—whatever they have learned or received." (Phil. 4:9)

If your church has a strong small-group ministry, consider ways to get every small group to adopt a specific church ministry partner. Adoption should include praying for, corresponding with, and providing transportation and housing for missionaries when they visit your church. Just think how much more support a ministry partner has when they know a group of individuals are lifting their specific needs up in prayer on a daily or weekly basis. Life Group ministry partner adoption allows people to become intimate with the ministry partners your church supports and allows them to participate in the blessings of the missionary.

Another way to get the church small groups involved in outreach is to help them get involved in a local community project. At my last church, we called them Adopt-A-Community projects. Almost every area of a city or town has communities that could use a helping hand in fixing up the neighborhood, doing feeding projects, or helping to run community centers. Challenge your small groups to look for neighborhood improvement projects that they can help out with. You can give them a head start by contacting local city council members or county supervisors to find out the needs of specific areas, and share those needs with the small groups. They do the work while your team plays the role of facilitator.

One way to get the whole church involved in missions is for the church to adopt a people group. There are a number of ministry agencies that participate in this program (listed on my Web site). You can learn more about this program at www.adopt-a-people.org. There are a number of ways you should consider when selecting the people group that you believe God wants you to adopt.

First, your entire team and church leadership should be involved in extensive prayer as to which unreached people group God would choose for your congregation. Look for the natural bridges that exist between your congregation and a particular people or area of the world. Are there any natural connections that already exist with a particular group or country? Perhaps it might be a people group that an existing ministry partner is already working with. Your team or your lead pastor might also have a vision or burden for a particular area.

You need to also pay attention to any particular nationalities that live in the vicinity of your church. Would it make a connection with those people if your church were involved in outreach in their country? Also consider if you have any strong people-group interests that already exist in the church. Another approach could be to consider where the church has already gone on short term mission trips.

Make sure you have your elder and pastoral staff involved. This helps lay the foundation for further involvement and participation on their part and will help strengthen the relationship between leadership and the team. Solicit the advice of churches that have a successful adopt-a-people program or have previously done an adoption. Make sure you are aware of any security problems related to communication or travel to a particular area. There are still a number of countries whose borders are closed to Christian missionaries (from inside and outside of the country).

Another way to get your church involved in missions is to adopt a sister church of another ethnic group or inner-city area. Pastors and worship teams could exchange pulpits once or twice a year, and the two churches could learn from one another. It would expose your congregation to another culture, or at the very least a different income level. Down the road, you could consider jointly led short-term trips to their native country. It would also be a way to potentially bless another congregation and help them with any difficulties they face. Once a year, you could have a combined ministry event or picnic with the other church.

Once you have generated more missions interest in the church, then your next task would be to create a climate where every church ministry might go on a short term trip each year. The missions department should become the facilitator for training and orientation for all of the other ministries who actually create the short-term trips. The nice thing about this idea is that you could facilitate trips with a specific ministry focus and also create some potential ownership of projects by other ministries.

For instance, let's say that your team recently approved a project for building a Christian school in Africa. Once built, the only recurring cost would be the financial support of a teacher or teachers and perhaps some school supplies. You could work with the women's ministry team to share information and updates about the project and encourage them to "adopt" the funding of the teacher support and supplies. This would be something they would take ownership of with the missions team's oversight. Then, every few years, you could send a small women's ministry team to visit the school and surrounding area to look for more outreach opportunities. And it could grow from there.

Speaking of trips, too many missions teams don't make the best use of their missions festival to promote short-term ministry trip opportunities. Often the festivals are used to share trip reports, but those should be saved to create additional opportunities to share and highlight missions throughout the rest of the year. You should use your missions festival to announce all of the short-term missions trips for the following year. It's a way to generate interest and participation in the trips, and you can encourage signups for the trips during the festival, which in turn should promote higher support.

Another idea would be to create a "Vacation with a Purpose" program that would give individuals in the congregation access to many other short term mission opportunities around the world. Many times, having someone from your church join a completely different team with an agency you don't currently partner with can lead to new relationships with other ministries you may not have known anything about.

You could also create an individual Adopt-A-Missionary Prayer Program, with signups during your mission's festival. While getting your small groups to adopt a ministry partner is a great idea, you don't want to leave out all those individuals who for whatever reason don't belong to a small group. Help them become prayer warriors and give them an opportunity to be involved in your ministry partners' lives.

You could have a massive signup board where people could place their names below a specific ministry partner and the country they work in. Then you could have a separate sheet where they could list their personal contact information. All commitments would be for one year. All you have to do is create separate e-mail distribution lists for each ministry partner and forward their updates to everyone who has signed up to support them. Just imagine what could happen if your ministry partners were covered by everyone in your church!

Many church members aren't comfortable traveling to foreign lands and Third World countries or simply don't feel called to participate on short-term trips. While you should never give up on encouraging them to participate in a life-changing experience, you can create local outreach opportunities that will put their hidden gifts and talents to work just as well.

You could work with your local school district to create a citywide elementary and junior high school tutor network. If members feel uncomfortable working with children, then create or help them get involved in food collection or distribution programs to low-income neighborhoods. You could create a clothing collection program at the church, with weekly or monthly collections. You could make them aware of opportunities in local community centers or create neighborhood clean-up projects.

The opportunities are endless—all you have to do is make sure they're planned and executed responsibly and properly. Have a point person for each program who is willing to take ownership of it. Your role as a team should be to facilitate and participate in the programs, not necessarily lead every one of them.

Often overlooked in ministry promotion is the need to send out thank-you cards or letters on a yearly or even quarterly basis, thanking people for their funding support and encouraging them to continue to be involved. You should briefly outline where the money went or the results it produced, and attach it with a self-addressed, stamped postcard to solicit "opportunities for improvement" in addition to contact information for future involvement. You could create a checklist of different potential ministry opportunities they might want to be contacted about as new programs become available.

Thanking people and giving them the opportunity to give you feedback lets them know you care. Sure, you expose yourself and the team to some potential negative feedback too, but by opening yourselves up, you become reachable and relatable. When people know you care, they're more inclined to listen when you share. Don't be afraid to solicit feedback and always take the time to respond to concerns. It will always pay off in the long run, and you set a great example of a caring Christian.

Increasing Support

The emphasis of this strategy component is specifically designed to increase support of the missions program not only financially but also in prayer. The strategy needs to address members of the congregation as well as church leadership and pastoral staff.

Encourage your leadership team to include sermons on missions, evangelism, and how to be salt to the world when they map out their curricular approach for the year. This would be in addition to the standard annual missions festival sermon each year and could emphasize leadership's commitment to missions and the opportunity for all members to be involved. The idea is to find a way to bring missions out of the closet more than once a year.

Remind and encourage your teaching pastors to pray for and encourage support for your short-term missions teams and ministry partners. Share with them what an encouragement it is to your short-term teams to be prayed over publicly by them or the church leadership. Ministry partners should be included during prayer at weekly pastor meetings. You could also hand out a weekly prayer need summary sheet for your ministry partners that could be prayed for by the elder board or pastoral staff on their own time.

Create a simplified brochure titled along the lines of: "Missions: How Can I Help?" that contains ways for church members to get involved in missions without necessarily having to join your Global Ministry Team. It could include hosting a missionary in their home and giving them a place to stay when they visit your church. Those who have a gift for hosting will have an opportunity to create new and lasting friendships.

You could encourage church members to invite a missionary to their small-group meetings. Let them know that your global ministry partners enjoy sharing their ministry news and that their groups can learn first-hand the challenges your ministry partners face and the results their efforts have made with the blessing of God. It could also promote child sponsorships in Third World countries with the many quality Christian organizations that are looking for sponsors to help support needy children. This brochure could be a handout at your ministry table and duplicate the "How can I help" Web page you design.

If your missions budget operates on a faith promise, consider sharing potential future ministry projects prior to your faith promise request. This would allow your global ministry team to share a vision of the potential impact your church might have as a congregation in the coming year. The ministry partners or projects mentioned would already be tentatively approved by your team and church leadership (with no actual final financial commitment made).

This is a uniquely different approach to faith promise fundraising. Most churches rely only on past achievements to raise money in missions, but that only gives your congregation half the picture. Consider this: if you go to a bank for a loan, they not only consider your past financial history, they want to know what you are going to do with the money if they approve the loan. People are no different. This would create a two-pronged approach that would allow your team to also paint a picture of how the church might partner with ministries and participate in the blessing that God has in mind for them in the coming year. People need to be led; they need to see a vision.

Celebrating Results

This is perhaps the most important strategy component of the four, but it is often the most overlooked. Many times, churches do a really good job in missions but fail to let anyone know about it. If more people knew what kind of work was going on and the results that were being achieved for God's kingdom, more people would support and participate in missions.

When the prophet Habakkuk complained to God about the leaders of Judea oppressing the poor, he did so out of concern. He couldn't understand why God could allow this to happen because he could not see God working. God responded to Habakkuk that those who have faith in God would have the assurance that He was doing what was right. He assures Habakkuk, "For the earth will be filled with the knowledge of the glory of the Lord." (Hab. 2:14)

After hearing this from God, Habakkuk offers a prayer of praise. He prays, "Lord, I have heard of your fame, I stand in awe of your deeds, O Lord. Renew them in our day, in our time make them known." (Hab. 3:2) If Habakkuk's faith was renewed by what he heard from God, just imagine if he could have seen what God was going to do. We have the wonderful opportunity to not only let people hear what God is doing in His kingdom; we can also help people see what He is doing.

I'm continually surprised at how many churches don't provide some time to inform members of their congregation what took place on a church-supported short-term missions trip.

For one thing, did everyone come back healthy and okay? What was accomplished? Did it lay the groundwork for another trip? How did the trip impact the team members personally?

You see, there is absolutely no reason that a five- to ten-minute trip highlight segment can't be planned into a program weeks in advance. Many pastors who hold multiple services on Sunday mornings have a right to be concerned about clock management—within reason. Perhaps on that Sunday, the worship band plays one less song and the sermon lasts thirty-five minutes instead of forty to make room for some missions time.

This sends a direct message to the congregation that this trip was important and that participation in one is a special thing. It also provides a golden opportunity to ignite the desire to participate in other church members' hearts. Some churches allow a special breakfast or luncheon for trip highlights, but those generally only attract team supporters or missions junkies. While there is nothing wrong with these events, they should be in addition to a general assembly time, not instead of. After all, this should be something to celebrate!

Returning trip members should also be coached on how to relate their experiences on the field to others in the congregation. If they are going to be given the opportunity to share a trip experience or give a testimony in front of the congregation, they need to consider the time allotted to the entire team and focus on one event and one relationship that really stood out. If someone asks them, "How was your trip?", they should reply, "It absolutely changed my life!"

At the very least, try and get church leaders to set aside time for a fully produced three-to five-minute trip highlight video. It should have a carefully scripted voice over and have background music that will create a greater sense of impact when combined with the images on the screen. The video should focus more on the needs of those visited and what was accomplished than on the team members who actually went on the trip. Too many times, trip videos focus on the team members. You see them giggling and waving and having a great time, but you don't gain any sense of what actually was accomplished or how lives might have been changed. Now I'm not suggesting that everyone look serious and morose when being filmed, but that the focus should be on the mission, not the missionaries.

With the improvement in communications technology, some of the more techno-savvy churches are sharing trip highlights via live video feed while the team is still on the field. This is a great way to introduce people out in the field to team members helping from home. It gives congregation members a better chance to relate to what is happing on the field. Many times, a person's empathy towards the plight of others leads to a desire to get involved.

Another way to celebrate results in a more subtle manner is to create a missions wall map that not only shows the locations of all of your ministry partnerships but also allows a space in each ministry location to show ministry results that are updated on a monthly basis. This could contain information on people coming to Christ, children fed through a feeding program, medical outreach done, buildings built or fixed, discipleship groups meeting (new or totals), Gospel shared, people baptized, etc. Keep the information simple (no paragraphs) and in large enough type that people can read it without reaching for their bifocals.

Another idea that can make a real impact on people is to create a giant thermometer or graph that illustrates a running total of all of the people who have come to Christ as an indirect result of the ministry partnerships or projects your church supports. You could also create a giant heart that is being filled up with color representing God's heart and the people coming to Christ as a result of church support and participation. These only need to be updated once a year, but should be posted prominently on a wall for all to see.

Now, some people might look at this as showing too much pride, but I don't agree, if it is presented in a way that shows humility. The information should promote the partnership and support, not take credit. Done well, this can really make a point of letting people know your church is serious about the Great Commission, especially newcomers visiting your church for the first time.

You should also replicate this type of idea in the missions area of your church Web site. I would suggest creating a running summary highlight page dedicated to sharing all of the ministry partners you added, the significant results they achieved, and projects your church was directly involved with or supported financially. The page could be in a running scroll format or feature the graph, thermometer, or heart as your cover page with individual pages dedicated for each specific year your church has been involved in missions.

Last but not least, make sure to hold a missions festival at least once a year. This is a an excellent opportunity to bring in guest speakers, ministry partners, display items from other countries, share food from other cultures, and most importantly celebrate results. Every missions festival should have a theme and a Bible verse that underscores the purpose of that year's festival.

Consider displaying flags of all of the countries where you had ministry partners. (If possible, those flags should be left up year-round for all to see.) Each year, hang banners near the church entrance or inside the sanctuary that highlight the theme for the festival and the supporting scripture. You could also create banners (rotated weekly) that present missions "food for thought" such as these:

"We are created to Glorify God"

"We Glorify God by loving others"

"This is how they will know us"

"We are blessed to be a blessing to others"

"God is on a mission to save the world and invites YOU to join Him"

"God is on a mission to save the world. So, what are your plans today?"

"We are created to worship God. Are you fulfilling your destiny?"

"Expect great things *from* God. Attempt great things *for* God."

"Go into all the world and preach the good news. Any questions?"

"God has a plan to save the world. How do you fit in?"

Your lead pastor should be deeply involved with this festival. He needs to play an important and active role in promoting the festival ahead of time and encouraging members to come and be involved. This is no time for the lead pastor to take a vacation! A flyer should be sent out to all church members ahead of time promoting the festival, inviting them, and encouraging them not to miss out on all of the excitement. That's the key—your missions festival has to be fun, exciting, memorable, and most importantly strategic.

Consider having the high school or junior high ministries perform in missions skits. Get the children's ministry involved and make sure that the missions theme is incorporated, promoted, and taught in classes during that time period. Have the younger children create a missions countdown starting a few weeks ahead of the missions festival.

I would also suggest creating a "Missions in Action" brochure that is handed out to everyone. It should detail the theme of the festival and contain in-depth information on your ministry partners (including photos), along with highlights and achievements from that year's global ministry participation. It may seem redundant, but make sure these brochures are available the rest of the year after the festival so people who missed out on the festival or are new attendees have a chance to learn about your global ministry program.

If possible, have your ministry partners send you brief one- to two-minute videos of what they are doing on the field and possibly thanking the congregation for their support. These could be tied together into a larger video or used separately throughout the Sunday morning program or on successive weekends if the missions festival is a part of a faith promise campaign.

If you are able to have ministry partners available for the festival, introduce them and either let them share testimonies of their ministries or give them tables or booths where they can share their ministries and display unique items from the countries they work in. You could create games where church members have intriguing question cards or sheets that can only be answered by the ministry partners at their booths. Consider tying in the completed game cards as a meal ticket for the cultural festival food you might serve. This helps place more focus on the ministry partners than the food that people will naturally rush to devour after service is over.

If this seems like too much focus on food, consider going in the opposite direction by asking church members to fast and pray. Then you could use the opportunity to teach about hunger worldwide.

This is also a good chance to have the worship team get involved and present worship music with a distinctly different flavor. You could look at having your worship pastor invite the worship team from an ethnic Christian church in your community to perform the worship music for the festival. It's another great way of making members of your church aware of other cultures in your community.

You might consider having your lead pastor or special missionary guest report on worldwide missions activity continent by continent and share how many new people have come to Christ or were baptized, disciple, or fed. You could also report on how many new churches were planted. This can be as inspiring to your visiting missionaries as it is to members of your church.

The key is celebration. A missions festival is a time to give praise and glory to God for all the great things He is doing in this world, despite what a negative press tells us every day. David summed it up best in Psalms 145:10–12:

> *All you have made will praise you O Lord; your saints will extol you. They will tell of the glory of your kingdom and speak of your might, so that all men may know of your mighty acts and the glorious splendor of your kingdom.*

And isn't that what it's all about?

Last but not least, I would suggest that you might create a format to allow the congregation to positively and constructively critique your annual missions festival. Enclose a simple questionnaire in the Sunday bulletin a week after the festival that members can drop in a box at the exits, or you can send it out in the mail as a self-addressed, pre-stamped postcard that members can send back. Keep it limited to three or four questions such as:

1. Did you enjoy this year's guest speaker?

2. What did you like best about this year's festival?

3. What did you find the most intriguing?

4. What could we do to improve the festival next year?

As I mentioned earlier in the book, opening your ministry up to constructive criticism shows the congregation you care, and they will be much more likely support your future promotions. For many church members, missions week is a time to skip out because after all, it's only going to lead to the church asking for money to support missions, right? I'll say it again: they have to know you care before they want to hear what you have to share.

CHAPTER 7

▼

FUNDING YOUR MISSIONS PROGRAM

There are many schools of thought on how much money is needed to properly fund the work of the Christian missions workforce in the world today. Obviously the more funds we raise, the larger the workforce could be and the more projects could be funded. But the problem isn't so much that we need to raise more money, it comes down to how and where those funds are invested. If more missions funding were actually directed toward the unreached, perhaps more people would know the Gospel of Jesus Christ.

That said, the average Christian church in America today is falling far short in its responsibility to teach the biblical aspects of tithing. When it does fulfill its responsibility, it generally does a poor job of investing those funds to reach the world for Christ. We would have plenty of money to fund all the needed Christian missions work in the world if the people who fill the pews would give faithfully and the money was invested wisely.

The other problem we face is with missions stewardship. Sometimes churches that are blessed with larger budgets become more relaxed in how they appropriate their funds, and that can lead to waste. While we should never operate out of fear for making a mistake, we need to be diligent in our funding methods and hold ministry partners or agencies accountable for making the most from that funding.

Jesus taught a great lesson about waste in the book of John when He fed the five thousand on the shore of the Sea of Galilee. It's a lesson many readers overlook because attention is naturally drawn to the miracle of the loaves and fish.

> *When they had all had enough to eat, he said to his disciples, "Gather the pieces that are left over. Let nothing be wasted." So the gathered them and filled twelve baskets with the pieces of the five barley loaves left over by those who had eaten."* (John 6:12–13)

If Jesus had the power to multiply two fish and five loaves of bread to feed five thousand, why would He be so concerned about saving the scraps? Perhaps He wanted to save it to eat later, or have it in case He and his disciples ran into other hungry people later on the road. The key here is that He was making a point about wastefulness. Jesus was never one to overlook an opportunity for a teachable moment, and this event certainly was no exception. He wanted his disciples to realize that everything God provides is precious and should be viewed that way.

Many people complain that they can't give what they want to because they are mired in an endless cycle of debt created from wanting bigger and better things in life. The Gospel of Christ has literally been hijacked by the need to pay off personal debt. But has it really? According to most of the major missions think tanks, it is estimated that about 18 percent of all American Christians give to the cause of missions on an annual basis, which represents an average of around $300 per household per year. If we take things further, that total represents less than a dollar per day.

So for the sake of argument, let's set a paltry, low benchmark average of one dollar per day ($365 per year) for every regular attendee in your church. What would those numbers look like? Basically, if you work for a church of 1,000 regular attendees, your missions program should be raising and giving at least $365,000 per year towards global evangelization, and at least 18 percent of your congregation should be involved in the giving. A church with 3,000 members should be giving at least a million dollars per year to missions with the income coming from at least 540 people. But most churches would fall way short of that benchmark.

Occasionally, you will hear the names of famous missions churches with million-dollar missions programs, and everyone says "Wow, that's incredible. Those guys really rock for missions!" And that truly is a wonderful thing. But a closer look reveals a church with 5,000–6,000 members who are underperforming by at least 50 percent of what they could or should be doing using the extraordinarily low benchmark set above.

So how does your program compare? At the last church whose missions program I led (using the principles contained in this book), we had a faith promise budget of $225,000 with a congregation of about 250 regular attendees. That's close to $1,000 per person, and we were a very ethnically diverse, mixed-income church. If you think about it, that's still less than three dollars per day per person. Now the reality was that the funds we raised came from commitments from roughly half our congregation. That's closer to $2,000 per person who donated. So let's set that as another benchmark to shoot for: at least 50 percent of your congregation gives to missions. It's not impossible; it can and has been done.

I realize that most missions leaders have a passion for missions, not for raising money. But it is important that not only church members but also church leaders understand the need for world evangelization and our responsibility to complete the Great Commission. They need to be encouraged, and you have to be persistent. You have to take the necessary steps, even if you have to begin with baby steps. A dollar per day and 18 percent participation is all you need! If you are achieving these kinds of numbers, don't pat yourself on the back just yet. Remember, these are the minimum numbers to shoot for. If you really want to think your missions program is big-time, aim higher.

That said, how should you fund your missions program? There are five basic missions funding methods: general fund designation, faith promise, combined unified giving, individual designations and cooperative church consortiums. These funding methods vary in their quality and effectiveness, so I will break them down for you to help you consider which one (or combination) might be right for your church and missions program.

Types of Funding Programs

General Fund Designation

This funding method eliminates the need for asking for separate donations for missions from the congregation. It also means that missions funding is decided by church leaders, not the members of the congregation. Some people like this approach because they believe it guarantees funding for missions, but the question becomes how much of the church budget will be designated for missions. What is "missions" in the eyes of the church leadership?

Often I hear pastors or church leaders using this method say, "We give an honorable tithe to our missions program." What exactly does "honorable" mean?

A tithe is a tithe. Can a tithe be less than 10 percent? I know of many churches operating on a faith promise program whose program funding would be shattered if they only received a tithe of the general budget. The Bible mentions at least three different tithes in the Old Testament: a tithe to God for supporting His work (Lev. 27:30–32), a tithe to provide for God's people to observe His commanded festivals (Deut. 14:22–23), and a tithe every third and sixth year of a seven-year cycle to help the poor and needy (Deut. 14:28).

Some people assume that just one tithe was saved and then divided by the person among these three categories as he saw fit, but the Bible's instructions contradict this assumption, and there is nothing written in the New Testament that abolishes what was written in the Old. In fact, Jesus backs up the teachings of the Old Testament in Matthew 23:23. He chastises the Pharisees who were only tithing their spices and holding back their money for more important matters:

> *Woe to you, teachers of the law and Pharisees, you hypocrites! You give a tenth of your spices—mint, dill and cumin. But you have neglected the more important matters of the law—justice, mercy and faithfulness. You should have practiced the latter, without neglecting the former.*

So how much of the budget should go to missions? Using the above multiple tithing formula, one might assume at least 23 percent per year. I think a better question would be, what does your church leadership think is honorable to God when funding missions? There are churches out there that are giving almost 50 percent of their general budget to missions. Under this funding method, those are the real all-stars. If you use this type of system, it's important to work patiently with church leaders, encouraging them to increase the percentage assigned to missions from the general fund each year.

Faith Promise

This approach to missions fund raising was started over one hundred years ago. It is the method of choice used by some of the healthiest mission churches in North America. Once a year, you ask each member of the congregation to prayerfully set an amount that they believe God will enable them to give, above and beyond their normal tithing to the church. They place that amount on a card that is turned in with the weekly offering. Some individuals give a one-time gift, some make out a monthly check, and others give to their commitment every week. Normally, about 90 percent of Faith Promise commitments are realized.

Some church leaders get concerned that the Faith Promise will affect their general fund giving, but most churches have found that general giving tends to increase with an increase in missions giving. If they're not sure, ask them to give a call to leaders of churches who use a Faith Promise. What's nice about a Faith Promise system is that it helps to actually teach the meaning of faith by encouraging expectation and trust in God's provision.

You need to set a budget goal based on the needs of the ministries you support or the new opportunities you have discovered that your church might participate in for the coming year and share those needs to the congregation. Your team should prayerfully consider what that budget should be on a yearly basis, submit it to the church leadership for their approval, and then present it to the rest of the congregation.

A Faith Promise system creates a clear, defined line between the general fund and a fund specifically for missions. It makes missions a congregational issue that allows missions funding to be considered by every member. You can also use a Faith Promise card to confidentially invite, receive, and track commitments for support, prayer, and ministry participation.

Combined Unified Giving

This funding system provides for a General Fund Designation, and also allows members to give a Faith Promise to add to the amount going to missions. This system is often used by churches as a way to fund missions while they transition from a General Fund Designation into a Faith Promise program. It is also used by churches that are just getting started in missions and are a little nervous about how it might affect their general budget.

Many times churches will use their General Designation Fund to support ongoing ministry partners, and then allow for special fundraisers to support specific missions projects or a Faith Promise that will go towards a specific program or programs that members might wish to support in addition to their regular tithing.

Individual Designations

This system is used when a church approves individual missionaries then encourages the congregation to support those missionaries by asking them to designate their support for those individuals they feel led to support. This method can give people a sense of ownership with their missions money, but it can also create a formidable challenge for the bookkeeping staff that has to track all of the individual donations, especially in a large church. You also have to figure that you will need to allow a greater part of your general church budget for administration to keep track of all those records.

Cooperative Church Consortiums

This can be advantageous for a number of churches who are still supporting the outmoded paradigm of supporting mainly homegrown missionaries. The idea here is that a number of churches work together and pool their funding so that new missionaries can raise their individual support in a shorter period of time. It also benefits the missionaries when they come home for furlough, because all of their support churches are in close proximity of each other. This method allows individual churches to pool their resources to participate in missions projects that they would not have been able to participate in otherwise.

The negative side of this funding method, though, is that it requires everyone to agree on most aspects of missions investment, which is not an easy thing for anyone to do, even if they are Christians. It also requires a considerable amount of work and administration by a church that everyone trusts within the group, unless everyone can agree on specific roles for their respective churches. This system has been used with positive results for a number of churches willing to work together.

Presenting Your Missions Budget

No matter what type of funding method is used, you will always need an element of public relations savvy to inspire church members to support missions. The key is to communicate effectiveness, not just finances. You have to remember that every day, church members are bombarded on TV, by mail, and via the Web with advertisements and solicitations to support hundreds of worthy causes around the globe. Your global ministry team has to show it is more effective with what is entrusted to them than the other causes.

It is important to honestly and consistently present a subtle message that the ministries and projects you support are achieving the results that are expected of them, and that what they do is glorifying God. You have to remind church members that they are an active participant (both financially and prayerfully) in the Great Commission and that God delights when they are faithful and He is glorified.

When you do present a budget or funding need to your congregation, it should focus on the needs of your ministry partners and the potential projects the church could either support or be involved in. This presentation should always be accompanied by an insert in the Sunday church bulletin or in an extra handout that church members can take home and study. If you present things well, you will usually get a really good response.

If you use a Faith Promise funding program, you have to be willing to set a budget goal based not only on your expectations for commitments during the fund raising campaign, but on the amount you think God will place in your trust by the end of the budget year twelve months later. If you church is doing a good job reaching out to the community and attracting newcomers and you are doing a good job keeping the congregation updated, more people will give to missions during the year. In this way, your team is also practicing a faith promise in that you set your budget not based on what you think the membership is willing to give, but rather what God will provide throughout the year.

It's also important to remember that once you have an approved budget in place and commitments have been made that you update the church membership on the status of that budget on a regular basis. It can be either weekly or monthly, depending on how sensitive church leadership is about sharing these updates. I always say people won't know there is a need until they are informed of one. You should try to have a space set aside for a weekly statement in the church bulletin of the total dollar amount given and needed, which should be broken down for a year-to-date total as in the example below:

Missions Budget

(4/1/05 to 3/31/06) 321,092

Faith Promise Cards Received 291,092

Additional Gifts Needed 30,000

Budget Year-to-date 85,004

Given year-to-date (98.5%) <u>83,786</u>

Variance—1,218

Keeping your congregation informed and updated about your missions budget on a regular basis also helps prevent the need for you or any other church leader to appear in front of everyone to make a stronger appeal to support missions halfway through the budget year.

Occasionally you will find yourself needing to step forward and make an appeal to the membership to remind them of the missions commitment they made earlier in the year.

When that happens, consider sharing how Paul encouraged the church in Corinth:

> *Now finish the work, so that your eager willingness to do it may be matched by your completion of it, according to your means. For if the willingness is there, the gift is acceptable according to what one has, not according to what he does not have." (2 Cor. 8:11–12)*

Raising funds to support your program is a necessary part of building a good missions program that will bless people. The money is there; you just have to ask for it. God provides worms for birds to eat, but He doesn't throw them in their nests! Faith by its very nature must be tried before the reality of faith is experienced.

CHAPTER 8

▼

CREATING A MISSIONS-MINDED CHURCH CULTURE

No matter how mature or missions-minded a church thinks it is, there will always be new people entering through the doors who know nothing about God's call to missions. Unfortunately, there are many mature Christians who still haven't grown enough in their faith to become "World Christians." They just can't seem to catch a vision for missions.

Missions needs to be caught, not just taught. People have to sense that the whole church is passionate about missions. As I said earlier in this book, you have to be careful to avoid a missions subculture within the church. The members of your team have to not only have relational bridges with those outside of the missions crowd, but also the church leadership and the rest of the pastoral staff. Community happens when there is a sense of celebration and relationship.

In life, we tend to support the people we love and people with whom we have a personal relationship. The same goes for missions. The more people love missions, the more they will support it. If the members of your missions team get involved in other ministries, they will make new friendships with other believers. Friendships foster trust, and trust means a lot when it comes to missions giving. Your team can't be viewed as a special interest group, nor should it be viewed as just one of many programs in your church. It's special, and it should be connected in some way with every other ministry in your church. In fact, it should be at the very core of everything your church does.

If possible, you should consider and seek out ways to get your ministry partners involved with the church membership on a more personal basis outside of sharing their ministries with the congregation. Consider having them speak at a function where missions is not the featured topic but perhaps an added value on a topic, such as at men's or women's retreat.

You might try and ask your ministry partners to share their heart for missions at a women's ministry luncheon or a men's breakfast. This way they're sharing not just the ministry but a way of life. How is God working in their lives, for instance? Perhaps it can be on Christian living topics and how these relates to their missions lives. This is a good way for church members to see the human side of missionaries and get a chance to know them better in a more intimate way.

Another way to build relational bridges with other ministries in your church is to make yourself or members of your team available to speak at other ministry events. The key is to create a number of messages that promote a missions viewpoint and relate it to people's daily lives. Of course, an occasional missions speech spiced up with wonderful stories from the field won't hurt, either. Also consider asking someone who has been on a short term trip to share their personal experience at different ministry events in the church.

Laying a Foundation for Missions

Before we can look at ways to excite and educate church members about missions and grow missions DNA, we have to look (at least briefly) at the larger challenge of creating mature Christians who will be open to hearing more about missions. Many churches today tend to treat a new believer coming to Christ as the end result, as opposed to the beginning of a lifelong journey—a journey filled with joy, but also a journey with expectations and responsibilities to God.

This is perhaps why we have so many "baby Christians" in the American church today. They came to faith ten or twenty years ago and have grown little in their faith to this day. Often coddled and never challenged to grow, they generally don't give much to the church unless it goes towards a program that helps them feel more comfortable. But there should be no spectators in God's kingdom, because of the one to whom much has been given (a new life in Christ), much is required.

Many churches have membership classes that new believers or attendees must attend in order to become church members. This is usually a single class that explains the basic purpose, rules, and policies of the church; once someone agrees to these fundamentals, they become members. I think more churches would be healthier today and get new believers or recent attendees off to a better start if the church created a series of required classes before one could become a member.

At the very least, churches could offer this series on a year-round rotational basis and make them available to all attendees. It could be set up as a quarterly program, with classes held successive weeks in a row, or on a monthly basis, where the entire series of classes would be offered twice a year. If this type of program were openly encouraged on a regular basis, it would eventually be a way of life in that particular church.

This short course could be very simple—maybe five different sixty- to ninety-minute classes offered on a monthly basis. The course could be called something like, "Growing in Faith." The classes would consist of the following and could be taken in any order: A foundations class, a worship class, a class on gifting, a missions class, and a final covenant class along the lines of "Understanding the Bible" or "Principles of Christianity," which would be a little more in-depth about principles of faith and could also include a missions mandate for your church.

Each of the five classes could have a deeper connected course that would be optional to all members and would last five to six sessions. This system would expose members to all of the longer in-depth courses and help whet their appetite for learning more. Some churches have a worship course, but unfortunately many of their members tend to think it's about learning to play music or sing as opposed to introducing people to the fundamentals and true meaning of worship.

The missions course could be a "Having a Christian World View," "Becoming a World Christian," or "Vision for the Nations" class. The missions and the worship class could be in sequence, since the whole reason missions exists is because worship doesn't. The Bible class could be something along the lines of "How to Read and Interpret the Bible" and could include ideas like the difference between an exegesis and eisogesis approach to the Bible and how to get the most out of God's word. While the mini intro gifting class would serve to help people discover their gifts, the longer "How to Use Your Gifts" class would cover all the gifts in-depth, what to do with them, and how to be a blessing with those gifts.

Churches shouldn't be afraid to also ask new members to consider volunteering for an area of ministry in the church. New believers need to understand that what makes your church special is that it consists of a body of believers who are committed to sharing and spreading the Gospel. It might seem heavy to some, but what type of members are you trying to attract, and what kind of believers are you trying to grow?

It's not like members have to commit to anything for life. If you create an environment that allows people to try different areas of ministry until they find one they enjoy, you will have a happier congregation who is more willing to serve, and your volunteer participation rate will probably be higher. This can serve as a great foundation for personal and spiritual growth. Ephesians sums it up best; it's what every church should be about:

But to each one of us grace has been given as Christ apportioned it. (Eph. 4:7)

It was He who gave some to be apostles, some prophets, some evangelists, and some to be pastors and teachers, to prepare God's people for works of service, so that the body of Christ may be built up until we all reach unit in the faith and in the knowledge of the Son of God and become mature attaining to the whole measure of the fullness of Christ. (Eph. 4:11)

Each of us has an obligation to prepare people for works of service so that the body of Christ may be built up. If a church reaches a unity in faith and in knowledge, it will become mature and, as a reward, attain the whole measure of the fullness of Christ. If it doesn't, that church might lose God's blessing.

Obviously you can never overlook leading new believers into the kingdom. After all, that's what missions is all about! But Jesus specifically commands us to also make disciples and teach them to obey everything He has commanded. We have to give believers the basic tools to understand and grow in their faith, and to take an active role in our church and God's kingdom. We then also need to give them opportunities to participate outside of church in the community and the missions field. We can't be afraid of helping people grow stronger in their walk. We may lose a few along the way, but the church in America will be stronger for it.

We need to help all believers understand key Christian concepts useful in their personal, family and business lives. Who am I as a Christian? What do I stand for? What is my purpose in God's plan? How do I maintain and grow my faith in this chaotic, unpredictable world (a good question for the eighteen to twenty-five crowd)? How can God infuse meaning into my life and my work? How do I remain renewed, engaged, and stimulated in my faith? How can I serve? Where should I serve?

As a community of churches, we need to look at what processes we can create that will help us build and grow Christians who have the foundation to develop a passion for missions. What type of enduring church does God want us to build? 2 Timothy 1:6–7 says it all:

> For this reason I remind you to fan into flame the gift of God which is in you for God did not give us a spirit of timidity but a spirit of power, love and self-discipline.

How to Grow Missions DNA

In the last chapter, I tried to address the touchy subject of raising funds to support your missions program. But there is something even more important to building your missions program than money: prayer. In fact, it's vital, and it should be your top priority. The importance of teaching prayer as a means of supporting missions cannot be overlooked. God was very specific about the church being involved in missions prayer and in Isaiah 56:7 said, "for my house will be called a house of prayer for all nations." Missions prayer should be the first step to being involved in missions for every church member.

It could start out as general missions prayer at first, then move up to prayerfully supporting individual ministry partners needs. If you operate on a Faith Promise, try to solicit prayer commitments on the fundraising card. This will allow you to measure how involved the church membership is in praying for missions. This is also a subtle way to show church members that prayer support is as important as financial support. As the prayer support for missions in your church grows, along with personal relationships between your team, ministry partners, and members, giving will naturally follow.

Again, try to get your church leaders and the entire pastoral staff to lead the way in missions prayer. Bring it up and include it at staff meetings. Send them prayer requests from your ministry partners and ask them to include them in their prayers. This has the added effect of informing church leadership and the rest of the pastoral staff of what is happening in the kingdom. It helps them to know your ministry partners on a more personal basis, too. Send them monthly missions praise reports from your ministry partners so they can be encouraged and share in the blessings of God's kingdom.

It's also important that your lead pastor helps to lead the charge when it comes to missions. In fact, this really is an absolute must. It has to be in his heart and something he believes in passionately, and you need him to actively support your team's efforts in front of the congregation. If not, you will have quite a challenge, unless you have a pastor who gives you complete autonomy as long as you do your job—and don't negatively affect the general church budget.

As you ramp up your efforts to build your missions program, encourage your pastor to write a short letter to the congregation sharing his feelings on the importance of supporting missions at least once a year. This is especially effective for a Faith Promise program when it is sent out a few weeks before a fundraising campaign starts. Sending one out before a missions festival is also helpful. If you can get your pastor and teaching staff to include missions in their sermons on a regular basis, even better.

Remember to be patient (something I'm personally not very good at). Building this type of support takes time. You need to weave it into the very fabric of your congregation. You and your team need to pray about it daily, plant seeds, and be prepared for the harvest. In his letter to teach Christians, James wrote:

> *See how the farmer waits for the land to yield its valuable crop and how patient he is for the autumn and spring rains. You too be patient and stand firm, because the Lord's coming is near.* (James 5:7)

It takes time, but God will reward your efforts, and your ministry will be blessed.

Building a Missions Education Program

Educating people about missions can be quite a challenge, but it is an important aspect of building a successful missions program and shouldn't be overlooked. Unfortunately, many people stereotype missions education as boring and repetitious. Much of the information is too detailed and mired in missiological terms that most people can't relate to. That's because it is usually presented in a boring manner by boring people. I'm sorry to say that, but sometimes the most knowledgeable people on missions are not the ones you want teaching it!

The key is to vary the way missions is taught and presented. Most people have built within them different learning styles that stimulate them to respond to information or ignore it. These four styles are analytical, common sense, dynamic, and innovative. It is important to develop and present missions education programs that employ each of these methods.

You need get creative when you present missions. It can be presented in skits that go with a weekly message, videos, films, slide shows, recommended books for the whole congregation to read, special guest speakers, prayer meetings, field trips, conferences, local outreaches, and at ministry breakfasts, lunches, or dinners.

Once you have a good foundational program in place, then you can begin to create opportunities for deeper missions education. I spoke earlier of a six-week foundational missions class. This class should be led by you or other missions team members and might also include a couple of guest speakers. While the first purpose of this class is to teach or remind church members of their obligations to share the gospel, it should also encourage them to learn more about missions and also whet their appetites for becoming more involved. This class should be weighted evenly between what has been done and what could be done in the missions field.

For those members that have a desire to learn even more about missions, consider promoting or even hosting the Perspectives on the World Christian Movement course. This course is an in-depth study on the history and purpose of missions. It is a pretty intense course that is held for four hours once a week for sixteen weeks with guest missions experts.

Each week's study includes reading a portion of the 780-page Perspectives Book and Study Guide and taking a two-page open-book quiz. The entire course prepares you for writing an in-depth thesis on evangelizing an unreached people group and then taking one full-scale final. Those who complete the course in its entirety and score sufficiently on the test are rewarded with a graduation certificate. The course can be used for college credits, though people have the option of just attending the course and listening to the speakers.

Teaching missions to your congregation shouldn't stop with adults; it should also include children. One of my "half" ministries I have been involved in for quite a few years is teaching Sunday school for grades K-5. It always frustrated me that none of the lessons we were asked to teach involved missions. The more I thought about it, the more I became convinced that children could and should be taught missions at an early age to develop a heart for helping others. In fact, we have an obligation to. Proverbs 22:6 says:

> *Train a child in the way it should go, and when he is old he will not turn from it.*

I developed a children's missions program called "Kids on a Mission" that basically walked our kids through the missions story of the Bible in twelve easy lessons. Each lesson also focused on the country of a particular ministry partner and included a memory verse, missions-related game, and a craft unique to that country. We also served up some unique snacks native to that country, if we could find them. I then developed missionary trading cards for each ministry partner that had their photo, a small country map, a few country facts, and then ways to pray for them and their country on the back.

I received permission from the wonderful children's pastor we had at the time to implement this program on the first Sunday of every month, and pretty soon the children were looking forward to their Missions Sundays. The key was getting the full and enthusiastic support of our children's pastor, then teaching the program to all of the volunteer teaching staff. It became a very successful program for us.

These are just a few ideas you might want to try to help your congregation learn more about missions. For some people though, there is nothing like experiencing missions first-hand to develop a heart for missions and a love for people from other cultures. Perhaps the most powerful source of missions motivation for many people is to actually visit the missions field. It can have a positive effect with any age group, so let's explore that next.

CHAPTER 9

▼

MISSIONS OUTREACH

It would be hard to argue the fact that nothing can make as big of a positive impact on a Christian believer as when they get involved in some form of outreach. It takes the attention away from their own problems as they discover and experience first-hand that there are many people worse off and in greater need than they are. I say that with a touch of humor, because most of us who live in the United States would hardly qualify as being in bad shape. Still, it's only natural that we get caught up in our daily problems, which come from the challenges of life itself.

But when we help others, something special happens. We develop empathy for what others go through on a daily basis, and we learn to think more about other people's welfare. In the course of doing so, we are able to attain a deep sense of satisfaction from the fact that we actually can make a difference in someone else's life. It feels good, and we want to continue doing it. In the process, our own personal challenges don't seem so big in the scheme of things.

Short-term missions trips provide an opportunity for people to grow in their faith like few other events. This is because most people have a built-in fear of missions. There are so many reasons for someone not to go on a missions trip: lack of time, lack of money, job conflict, health issues, prejudice, self-viewed lack of skills, language difficulties, heat, cold, different foods, strange smells, the length of trip, or a general fear of being outside of their personal comfort zone. When

people are able to overcome these obstacles and realize who helped them overcome it, they gain more confidence and grow in their faith.

That said, one of the most controversial topics in missions today concerns the
thing that missions is supposed to actually be about—missions outreach. More
debate is exercised over how much funding should go into outreach and the types
of outreach to be involved in than almost any other missions subject. It can
potentially have both a positive or negative effect on your overall program and
budget, depending on what you do.

A solid investment in short-term trips to other countries can have a positive
long-term impact on your missions program by creating more missions-minded
members in your church, who then have a tendency to give more financially to
missions. On the other hand, too many trips can bleed a missions program dry by
drawing funds away from much-needed field ministries that could really benefit
from more funding support.

It doesn't do any good to send church members all over the globe if at the end
of the day you have no money left to actually fund the ministries they were
involved in. The key is to find a balance. You have to ask yourself what the real
purpose is for these types of trips, and what the desired outcome is for your missions program.

Some churches are very involved in local outreach and use most of their
finances to fund foreign-based ministry partners. After all, it doesn't take sending
a group of people all the way to Africa at a cost of $3,000 dollars each to develop
a heart for helping others. But a global trip can have a dramatic effect on helping
them develop awareness and most importantly, a heart for other cultures. Ultimately you have to ask this fundamental question: how many people are coming
to Christ as a result of your outreach trips? Therein lays the challenge. Outreach
should be an important part of every missions program; you just have to decide
how much of a part because there is no one-size-fits-all answer.

There are pros and cons with every trip and every approach. I'll try to highlight them in an effort to help clarify some of the misconceptions that exist.
Regardless of which direction you decide to take, I will give you examples, obser-
vations, and suggestions to help you make this part of your program the most
effective it can be. One final suggestion: all trips should come with a standard dis-
claimer—"Warning: Our church is not responsible for powerful, life-changing
experiences as a result of these trips!"

Global Outreach

The Positive Side

George is a very successful doctor and businessman at a local church in the Northwest. His teenage son was developing a heart for missions through the high school ministry of the church, and he badly wanted to participate on short-term trip the church was organizing to Guatemala. He asked his father to come with him because of his medical expertise, and George thought it would be fun to go on a father and son trip together. Missions wasn't something George really had any time for or interest in, but the idea of spending some quality time with his son appealed to him, and George agreed to go.

After a few days of treating various minor injuries and maladies, a native from the local village came to him complaining that his bare feet were hurting him. Upon examination, George could see that the man's feet were literally rotting from a severe case of athlete's foot. The surgeon told the interpreter who was working with him to tell the man it was nothing that a can of foot spray and a pair of socks couldn't cure.

The interpreter relayed the message and told George that the man was so poor that he didn't own a pair of socks. The interpreter suggested that George might offer the socks he was wearing to the man. George was bewildered because his socks were sweaty and dirty from wearing them all day. He took them off and offered them to the man anyway.

Upon receiving them, the man burst into tears and hugged George, thanking him over and over again. George was so impacted by this display of gratitude that by the time he came back home, he was ready to give up his medical practice and other businesses to go into missions full-time. Fortunately, after speaking and praying at length with his missions pastor, George realized that God had given him a special gift and talent to be a successful surgeon and businessman and that his continued success could provide funding for many types of medical supplies and other projects, not just in Guatemala but around the globe.

The surgeon still has a very successful practice, but now he takes more time off to lead short-term medical outreach teams to Central America and fund needed missions projects in other countries, which helps share the love of Christ around the world. You can't put a price tag on that kind of life-changing experience. Everywhere he goes and with everyone he visits, George can't help sharing his newfound passion and experiences with others. He has now become an ambassador for Christ.

I'll never forget the personal testimony of a young man in his late teens who had gone on a short-term trip to Haiti with my first church. After having been their a few days, he apparently developed some irritable bowel problems. He described in complete seriousness and without any embarrassment how he was in the middle of a village with some other members of the team sharing the Gospel when all of a sudden he was hit with the need to take care of some personal "business."

He couldn't see a restroom anywhere he looked and was becoming desperate. At that moment, he decided to pray to God to help him locate a place to relieve himself. He opened his eyes and to his amazement he saw an outhouse where he was sure that there hadn't been one before. To him, it was a true miracle. The impact this moment made on him was incredible. His faith was strengthened beyond measure, and the impact his story had on his fellow Gen-Xers was amazing. He has participated on a number of short-term trips since and has developed true leadership skills for someone of such a young age.

Sometimes a short-term team can really kick-start a ministry in a new area through strategic outreach. I'm not talking about running from home to home sharing the Gospel in a village or building homes in Mexico that are immediately torn down and used for firewood once the team is gone. I mean meeting a specific need previously identified by the ministry partner working in a particular country that might be beyond the scope of what they are capable of doing.

This might include digging a well and laying pipe to bring fresh water to a village, medical outreach and community health evangelism, introducing a Sunday school curriculum to ministry leaders, building a ministry training center for church planters, Bible transport trips, or helping with a food outreach program after a national or regional emergency.

Another very valid reason for going on a short-term trip would be to investigate a potential new ministry partner for the possibility of investing in and supporting their ministry, or checking on the progress of an existing ministry partner. These types of trips should only require a few people at the most.

The Negative Side

I spent some time at a church whose missions program was really struggling to raise funds to meet the needs of their existing ministry commitments. They were doing so poorly in their fundraising efforts that they were receiving less than $200 per week in their Faith Promise program. Mind you, this was a church with an average attendance of five hundred people.

One weekend earlier, they had introduced to the congregation a team of eleven who were leaving for Ethiopia for a one-week feeding outreach trip at an orphanage. Being familiar with organizing trips to Africa, including Ethiopia, I thought, "Wow, that's probably a cost of at least $3,000 per person, for a total trip cost of $33,000 dollars." I later found out that the cost was closer to $4,000 per person (total trip cost $44,000), and that the church actually took two of these trips to Ethiopia per year and had been doing this for six years!

These trips were initiated by a loving, caring, dedicated woman, who had developed a passion for this particular ministry and had strongly encouraged the church to support the ministry partner who ran the orphanage. She genuinely believed she was serving under God's will to the best of her abilities. The church was now supporting the ministry partner with $9,000 per year. The church had also created an annual golf tournament, the proceeds of which were used to support the feeding program.

The week after the team came back home, different team members were brought up on stage to share their experiences and talk about how wonderful the trip was. The trip was great, the kids were great, we can't wait to go again, and you should come with us next time. (It turns out half of the team were repeat participants.) No one mentioned what or how the ministry was doing, how the ministry was changing the lives of the children, or why the church should support this ministry, outside of helping malnourished children. It was all about the team.

A week later, it was casually mentioned to the woman who spearheads this ministry that it was unfortunate that the congregation didn't get a chance to really learn anything more about the ministry or why the church should support it based on the team report. Most of the congregation already knew the church was supporting this ministry monthly and that children were being fed. It was just an accepted fact that this was something the church did.

What was missing was why this particular ministry was being supported and what purpose sending eleven people there twice a year helped to accomplish. She haughtily replied that this was her ministry, and the main reason she went on these trips twice a year was to make sure that the support money was being used properly.

My natural train of thought was, "Wonderful, this church is spending more than $80,000 per year to make sure $9,000 and change was being spent properly!" That made a whole lot of sense. Worse yet, when a ministry suddenly becomes "your" ministry, at some point it stops being God's ministry. When it no longer is God's ministry, how can you ascertain what God's will is?

Here we have a situation where you have a truly dedicated individual who has developed a passion for a particular people group. This is a person who in all likelihood introduced the concept of missions to this church in the first place. But in all of her passion, this earnestly caring woman had lost all sight of whose ministry it really was because she had become too personally attached to the ministry. Even worse, the church leadership had allowed her to literally hijack the missions program to support this particular ministry.

No one in leadership ever asked the question, "Is this the best way to bless this ministry?"

No one else on the missions team did, either. Perhaps the ministry could have served ten times as many children if all of the trip money had gone into the feeding program. Perhaps the team could have scheduled one trip per year and used the rest of the money for ministry support. This situation really helped highlight what happens when some people have more say on the team than others.

This ministry also highlighted other problems. No one could tell me what would happen to the ministry if the national ministry leader weren't around anymore. Was he grooming other national workers? Who would be responsible for feeding the children if he suddenly ceased to exist? Were the children being discipled to become young Christian leaders? Were they being educated, and how? What was the end result with these kids? Was any ministry replication taking place? Were there any plans to expand the ministry to other areas? Was this really a ministry or an expensive feeding program?

I then attended a missions team meeting at this church, and the team leader announced that the next church short-term trip was the annual sports ministry trip to Thailand. The cost was $3,000 per person, and the church was sending a team of at least eleven to play soccer with the "natives." I asked the ministry team leader if people actually came to Christ as a result of this ministry and if they tracked the results each year. She replied that they didn't track any results, but she figured a couple of people made a confession of faith each year.

I tried to explain as sensitively as possible that perhaps these trips were a large reason the ministry had so little money for actual "ministry." They would eagerly spend more than $33,000 to send a team of eleven to Thailand to play soccer in a sports ministry that nets two converts and feel great about it. Yet that same amount of money could have been used to support fifteen national church planters in Thailand or Mozambique for two years, which could lead to fifteen churches planted with an average of 50 to 200 baptized believers. That's 750 to 3,000 believers for the same amount of investment support.

Worst of all, the very nature of the trips and the way they were shared with the congregation did little to inspire the rest of the congregation to open their checkbooks and support the missions program. These three trips alone were potentially taking $110,000 out of the missions budget annually. After all, the money has to come from somewhere. That's more than half a million dollars in five years! Finally, because there were so many repeat trip members, the trips weren't having the type of impact on helping the church membership grow in their faith the way they could have. It had basically created a missions clique.

A while back, I was having lunch with the head of a missions agency that was heavily involved in training ministry leaders in church planting techniques in an extremely politically sensitive country. They had managed to get the leaders from a number of different protestant affiliations to all work together to win their country for Christ. These leaders have made incredible inroads in a fairly short amount of time.

Our church was a major supporter of the ministry leaders in this country. Despite the country being run by a dictatorship, they still granted a small number of ministry visas each year. The only way to get our funding support into the hands of the ministry leaders was when the ministry agency we worked with received these visas and then smuggled the money into the country to give to the leaders to support their ministries and help purchase supplies.

Unfortunately, another church in our area, which was heavily involved with an agency that specialized in creating short-term trips for churches, decided to send a team of door-to-door "evangelists" to this politically sensitive country. Until then, very few short-term teams had been sent to this country, and those that did go operated under the radar to support the ministry leaders in various ways that didn't attract any attention.

This irresponsible church and missions agency had decided that they could do a better job of sharing the Gospel than the national ministries who were working together and making tremendous progress. Armed with tourist visas, they invaded the country with a fairly large team, which entered local villages and went from door to door trying to share the Gospel.

Of course, it didn't take long for this team to attract the attention of the government, which was outraged by this above-ground display of Christian evangelism. It responded by complaining to the U. S. government and promptly canceling all future ministry visas into their country. The end result of all of this selfish behavior was that our church could no longer get funds through to these leaders. More than a year passed before the visa restrictions were lifted and our ministry partners could receive our funds to replenish their supplies.

I spoke with a couple of people who went on this high-profile trip, and they claimed that the team had led 1,400 people to Christ in a week. Oddly enough, the team went into areas that had already been evangelized. They weren't working with any local church, so assuming that they were actually successful doing something that the national ministries couldn't do, you have to ask the question, what happened to these people after they supposedly came to Christ? And what non national expert determined what area actually needed evangelizing?

There are a number of missions agencies that specialize in these evangelizing, short-term trips. In some cases, if working with a local church or ministry, a short-term team can come into an area and really kick-start a ministry. If someone does make a confession of faith, they can be given information about the local church or ministry where they can be discipled and grow in their faith. The local national church or ministry church in turn receives information about the convert from the team and can do follow-up visits with them. In this way, both sides compliment each other and positive results are achieved.

Short term ministry trips work best when they are initiated or requested by the ministry partner. They should be based on meeting the tangible needs of the ministry that operates in the native country, not on the needs or desires of your church. When churches request trips to "expand" the minds of their members, it forces the national ministry partner to spend their valuable time away from the main functions of their ministry in order to prepare for the team and create events that will keep the team busy.

Organizing Short-Term Trips

One of the ways to limit short-term trips' negatively impacting your missions budget is to make it a line item in your budget and assign a percentage to it. This is imperative if your church subsidizes short-term trips, but is still a wise thing to do even if it doesn't. The reason is that there is a finite amount of money that will be given to a church entity in a year by its members, and support for short-term trip members comes out of that. It is rarely an additional sum.

Once the total needed expenses of all combined trips reaches the budget limit of, say, 15 percent, no other trips are permitted for that fiscal year, barring emergency visits of individuals to ministry partners. The requested trips can then be set in a line of priority for the following year without hurting anyone's feelings. If you don't have them already, you should create written guidelines for trip organizing procedures that everyone in the church must adhere to.

The benefit for having these guidelines and a short-term trip budget line item (approved by church leadership) is that all trips then have to meet the criteria set by your missions team plus be approved by your team—period. This also forces better planning from other ministry leaders and prevents them from negatively impacting your missions budget. It allows all trips to be monitored by one entity, your team, and it prevents inner church politics from happening, where different church ministries compete with each other for team members and trip dollars. More importantly, it helps ministry trip leaders cut down on mistakes.

Ultimately, you want to your team to have the ability to schedule a series of trips each year and promote them at your missions festival as opportunities for the coming year. By working with the requests of other ministry leaders in your church and basing your decision on the needs of your current ministry partners or what your team is trying to accomplish, you can create a series of strategic trips that will meet your team's goals for creating more participation in missions without wiping out your ministry budget.

Short Term Trip Organizing Guidelines

Creating a good set of guidelines for short-term trip leaders allows them to work using a checklist and corresponding timelines. I recommend that a trip organizer contact your ministry team with a proposed trip at least twelve months in advance of trip date at the minimum. The trip organizer should communicate in writing the date and duration of the trip, along with the purpose and vision of the trip. They should be able to identify potential team leaders and the foreign contacts or global ministry partners the team will be working with.

Next, you want to encourage trip leaders to think out the mission of the team. How would they define a successful trip? Without setting goals, there is no way to measure if the trip was successful in its mission when it returns. They need to propose the size of their team and define the need for a team of that size. They should already have a complete trip budget and trip logistics (travel details, interpreter needs, medical concerns, and insurance requirements) worked out; otherwise, tell them to wait until the following year. Your role as a missions team should be to facilitate their trip, not do all of their planning for them.

You should than have them think through what their training needs might be. What evangelistic skills will they need? Will team members need other skills, such as medical, construction abilities, and will they need to work with an interpreter? How will the team leader promote team work, team harmony, and team member compatibility? Are they self-financed, or will they need help in learning how to raise funds for the trip?

Finally, the team leader should be able to clearly define how the team ministry vision fits in with the overall vision of your church and global ministry team. They should also be able to map out what their post trip plans are. How will they help team members download and process their trip experiences? How do they propose to share the experience with the rest of the congregation? These are all questions that should be answered at the time of the proposal.

You should then give your team at least thirty days to get together and discuss the merits of the trip and contact the team leader with your decision. If the trip is approved, the trip organizer should meet with your team to discuss plans and approve the leadership of team. At that point, your missions team should set and approve the minimum and maximum size of the team, in addition to the trip budget, with the team organizer.

Only after receiving approval from church leadership should the team organizer furnish copies of trip applications and criteria to potential trip participants. Your missions team can help promote the trip by ensuring that it is highlighted on your Web site, complete with downloadable trip applications and criteria, and through the use of church bulletin inserts.

Nine months before the trip date, the team leader or organizer should meet with your missions team to give an update and discuss potential team members (who have completed applications and turned in deposits), fundraising updates, and generally go over the progress of the trip. At that point, your missions team should approve or disapprove of the team members. Your team should maintain the right to approve trip members based on the needs of the trip, individual ministry skills, spiritual maturity, or past experiences with individuals.

Six months out, all trip participants should have at least 50 percent of their individual trip budget raised. The team organizer should be tracking these totals and provide you with a spread sheet of each trip member's fundraising progress. At this point, monthly team training meetings need to be initiated (with your missions team, if oversight is needed). The trip leader should now provide monthly e-mail updates to your team from this point on.

No later than ninety days from the trip date, the team members should have all of the money raised, valid travel documents, medical clearance, and any needed immunizations. Airline tickets and hotel reservations, if needed, should be purchased no later than this time. It should go without saying that the deadline for raising trip funds must coincide with airline ticket purchase. If a trip member is not fully funded, they don't go. If they raised funds instead of self-financing, the funds need to be returned to the people who donated.

Two months out, your missions team should have a final meeting with the team leader (or even the entire team) to get a final trip update and answer any questions they might have. At this time, each team member should be able to provide a list of prayer partners who will intercede daily on their behalf. This is a must, and it should be made clear ahead of time that any team member that does not have an intercessor team of at least ten or twenty people can't go on the trip.

A few weeks before the team leaves, the members of the trip should be brought in front of the congregation for a formal announcement of the trip. The team leader should be given a few minutes to present a brief description of the trip and a means of communication with the congregation while the team is abroad. The church leadership should also pray over the team in front of the congregation.

One week after the team returns, your missions team should meet with the team leader or trip organizer for a post-trip debriefing. A highlight meeting for the congregation should have been scheduled to be presented within two weeks of the return of the team.

Within a few weeks of their return, the team ministry leader and or your missions team should meet with the trip members to debrief them. Your team members should be available to help trip members process their experience, focus their thoughts, and discuss avenues for further missions involvement.

Along with general trip guidelines, you also need to consider having a missions trip filter that specifically addresses fundraising guidelines for team members along with individual responsibilities. This is especially important if your missions team subsidizes individual trip expenses out of your missions budget. Below is an example of what this might look like:

Missions-Minded Church
Short-Term Missions Trip Filter

Short-Term Missions Fund

The total budgeted fund will be divided by region as follows:

50%—Trips to unreached people group areas

30%—Trips to reached people group areas

20%—Trips to anywhere in the United States

Short-Term Trip Participants—MMC Support Funds

Unreached Areas w/MMC Ministry Partner: 30% Trip Support up to $300 per person

Unreached Areas w/o MMC Ministry Partner: 25% Trip Support up to $250 per person

Reached Areas w/MMC Ministry Partner: 20% Trip Support up to $200 per person

Reached Areas w/o MMC Ministry Partner: 15% Trip Support up to $150 per person

U.S. Areas: 10% Trip Support up to $100 per person

If the support request exceeds a specific region's budget, the available funds will then be divided equally between all trip team members. The remaining funding required for the missions trip must be raised by each team member.

Trip Participant Funding Breakdown

MMC Support Fund: 20% of total; Participant: 50% of remainder; Fundraising 50% of remainder

Examples:

Unreached Area: Trip Cost $1,500: MMC up to $300, Individual $600, Fundraising $600

Reached Area: Trip Cost $1,000: MMC up to $200, Individual $400, Fundraising $400

U.S. Area: Trip Cost $500: MMC up to $100, Individual $200, Fundraising $200

1.) Team members are required to pay 50% of their individual share as a deposit at the time of signing up for the trip. They are then required to: a) raise 50% of their total budget six months before scheduled trip; and b) complete all remaining fund raising 90 days before the departure date of the missions trip.

2.) All trip participants are required to send out at least 25 prayer or financial support letters within 30 days of signing up for the trip.

3.) Trip participants who fail to raise the needed funds within stated time periods will be dropped from the team and have their deposit refunded. Those who drop out of the trip after airline tickets are purchased are responsible for the cost of the ticket.

4.) Trip leaders or the missions team reserve the right to deny or remove a team member from a specific trip if individual's gifting is not appropriate for specific trip or the individual is in constant conflict with other team members and goals.

There are differing thoughts on whether churches should require trip members to raise all or a portion of their trip expenses from friends or the church membership. On one side, raising funds can make a team member more appreciative or humble in their attitude towards the trip, because they realize that they have been given an opportunity as well as a responsibility to serve well. The fact is, they wouldn't be going without the support of many people. On the other hand, you could be creating just another hoop to jump through or an impediment to getting people involved in short-term trips.

It's not that easy for a successful person who is well-off in life to go around asking for money when the reply from many will be, "You make enough money; why aren't you paying for it?" The downside of self-financing is that sometimes you will encounter someone with the attitude of "Hey, I paid for this, therefore I should be able to do what I want." My personal feeling on the matter is that a missions team should focus on making sure that funds are raised and not how the funds are raised. But that's just my opinion.

If you are going to allow or require trip members to raise funds, you should have a clear set of church leadership-approved fundraising guidelines available for all who need it. Below is an example.

Missions Minded Church
Individual and Group Fundraising Guidelines for Short-Term Ministry Trips

The purpose of these guidelines is to provide a clear understanding for all groups and individuals who wish to raise funds to support short-term mission trips and other ministry events.

Individual Fundraising

1.) All fundraising within the congregation must be done with people whom one has a personal relationship with. No random letter-sending or membership saturation mailings are permitted.

2.) Team or ministry members may not use the church database for soliciting support.

3.) Any funds designated specifically to support an individual team member will go toward that team member's individual trip expenses.

4.) No fundraising may be done without prior approval from church leadership.

Group Fundraising

1.) Students under the age of 18 may be allowed to raise funds by offering services or products in exchange for financial support. The price for products or services must be approved by the church leadership prior to the offering of services or product.

2.) All funds that are raised at group fundraising events shall be applied towards the team expense or ministry as a whole.

It is the desire of the Missions Minded Church Global Ministry Team to see all team members take personal responsibility for raising their own individual funds, and we encourage all team members to consider sharing their raised funds with other members who might have trouble raising funds for the good of the whole team.

Another area that your team should address with guidelines is financial support for pastors on trips, especially the lead pastor. More acrimony has been created between missions teams and their lead pastor because of this topic than almost anything else. Lead pastors get invited to participate on trips or attend and speak at conferences all the time. The question becomes, who pays for it—the pastor or the church? If the church is funding the trip, what part of church budget does the money come from, the general budget or the missions budget?

You might have a pastor who labels a pastor's conference in Sydney, Australia, as a missions field in dire need of his services in order to tap into missions funds and not affect an already strained general budget. On the other hand, a lead pastor, ministry leader, or missions team member that is asked to be a participant of a trip at the request of your missions team should not have to raise his or her own funds, since the request was generated by your team based on the need of a ministry partner or the team.

Here is a fairly good way to breakdown and clarify pastoral support for short-term trips:

Missions Minded Church
Criteria for Pastoral Support on Short-Term Trips

A. The MMC Global Ministry Team may propose or recommend that members of the Pastoral Staff participate on short-term missions trips. The goal of the trip must be to encourage and pastor our existing missionaries, support and build their ministry, teach or conduct training and discipleship programs, and engender accountability with our ministry partners.

B. The Global Ministry Team shall, if funds are available, support the pastor for 50% of expenses if the following parameters are met:

1. They are leading or actively participating on a short-term ministry trip that has been approved by the Global Ministry Team, and

2. The trip is in accord with the Global Ministry Strategy Plan, and

3. The purpose and itinerary is jointly established with the prospective traveler and the Global Ministry team, based upon the perceived needs at that time, and

4. Specific reporting venues would be established to report back to the congregation.

5. Funding of the trip would be dependent upon available Faith Promise funds.

C. If a member of the Pastoral Staff has been invited by an agency or another church to participate in a missions activity, or the focus of the trip is for building or casting vision, missions funds will not be allocated for such activity.

D. Members of the Pastoral Staff or Global Ministry Team who are sent on a missionary visitation trip at the request of the Global Ministry Team may be fully subsidized by the Global Ministry Budget, providing funds are available. These trips would need to involve visiting existing ministry partners in the field (due to accountability, communication, or personal problems) and/ or to provide pastoral care. These types of trips would only be considered as a means of last resort.

This specific document should be a policy document, not a set of guidelines, so there can be no gray areas subject to opinion or misunderstanding. Make sure you have it approved by your church leadership. Having a document like this will go a long way toward maintaining a great relationship with your lead pastor.

Last but not least, it is imperative that your missions team does its utmost to help facilitate and encourage trip members. Proverbs 15:22 says:

Plans fail for lack of counsel, but with many advisors they succeed.

Your team should be viewed as the ultimate resource for all things missions, and you should be able to readily equip short-term teams with trip supply checklists, missions travel agent contacts, and travel document requirements and information. You should also make yourself available to help teach trip members how to share their testimony, work with a translator, and learn subjects such as cultural awareness. If you cover all of the bases, you lay the foundation for a really successful short-term program.

Local Outreach

In the Book of Acts, Jesus instructs his disciples on how He wants them to witness the Gospel. He tells them in Acts 1:8:

And you will be my witnesses in Jerusalem, and in all of Judea and Samaria, and to the ends of the earth.

He wanted to impress upon his disciples that local ministry was as important as global ministry. Some churches divide local and global ministries into two different departments, but if local outreach falls under your responsibilities, consider yourself lucky. It can be a great training ground for people to develop a heart for missions.

Many times you have the opportunity to work with other cultures close to home. A trip to China, for instance, might offer an opening to work with a local Chinese Christian church in your town to reach those people for Christ. It can also lead to opportunities for mutual support of ministry partners, which can create long-term outreach partnerships.

Having people involved in local outreach opportunities allows you the chance to monitor potential global ministry team candidates as you support them and watch them grow in their faith. It also will show you if someone does not have the right attributes to serve in the missions field. If they create or have problems in a local ministry setting, those problems will manifest themselves tenfold in a foreign country.

Local outreach is as much about showing acts of human kindness as it is evangelism. Through our acts of kindness, people become interested in knowing why we do what we do, and they want to know more. Sometimes those acts of kindness come at just the right moment to make a dramatic impact on someone's life, and once they realize the source of that kindness, they want to have a personal relationship with Him.

The other great thing about local outreach is that it can completely change a non-Christian's viewpoint of the church. I often hear people comment that churches are all about taking people's money; these people are very surprised when they see or hear about a church giving back to the community. An effective local missions strategy should include acts of kindness and service in addition to support of worthy local projects.

At Silver Creek Church in San Jose, California, we had a woman who had become involved in a women's halfway home run by a local Christian agency. Through her concerns and efforts, our church basically adopted this place. We supported it financially and put on special events at different times of the year to share the love of Christ with the women staying at the home. One Christmas, members of the church all got together and donated enough artificial Christmas trees for every woman and her children to enjoy Christmas in their individual apartments for years to come.

One church I spent time with has a program called "Conspiracy of Kindness." Throughout the year, it schedules strategic outreach events in the community to show they care. The projects vary, from washing the windows of all the downtown businesses or cleaning and renovating people's yards to running a weekly food bank program or a volunteer-run thrift store whose profits all go to the missions program. Another church goes to homes of elderly people and shovels the snow in their driveway and sidewalks after storms. Yet another church cuts and delivers firewood to families that either can't afford it or aren't capable of chopping their own wood.

One great way to help the community is to organize and build a school tutor network.

Something that just about every school could use more of is volunteer tutors. All you need to do is contact the head of your local school district and find out where there is the most need. Most of the time, it will come from schools in the poorer side of town. This is a great way to get people from your congregation to step outside of their comfort zone.

Most tutoring programs can be set up very easily, with a group orientation run by the school district. Since the tutoring takes place after school at the same time for each grade, those that are nervous about going to a disenfranchised part of town can drive together and hold each other's hands! Get church members to sign up and commit to one hour a week. The commitments should run for the duration of the school year. If that seems like too much of a burden for some people, have them commit to twice a month but still for the entire school year.

The only issue you'll likely have with your local school district is to make them feel comfortable that your church members won't be evangelizing their kids. You have to build up a sense of trust. This is about helping others, not evangelizing them. Once they see that you don't have an ulterior motive, the door of opportunity opens even wider. You have to build up success.

The first year, you might concentrate on one school, then expand the program to others as more interest is shown. Once your tutors get involved in these children's lives, they will never be the same again. Your tutors need to share their enthusiasm with others in church and attract more volunteers. Then it's time to share your program with other churches and build an entire tutor network. Just imagine how the public will react when they find out district reading scores have been dramatically raised—and the reason for it is a Christian school tutoring network.

The greatest thing of all is that over time your tutors develop personal relationships with the children they tutor. The parents of the children begin to notice a positive change in their children's confidence and attitude about school, and it will create a natural desire to want to know more about the people who are helping their children. They will find out about your church without you even needing to tell them, and over time they might visit. So begins an exploration of faith, and you didn't have to go door to door proselytizing to do it.

Consider working with your city council member or county supervisor to adopt a neighborhood. Most cities have strategic neighborhood initiatives on the drawing board just waiting to be implemented. These neighborhoods are targeted for clean-up and beautification projects, drug sale and use elimination, safety improvement, community center building, and park additions. Since most city projects are understaffed and under-budgeted for these projects, your church can become the driving force for making those projects succeed.

Once involved in the community, your church can prayer-walk the neighborhoods and hold community events, such as host a barbecue, hold an Easter egg hunt, or organize back-to-school backpack giveaways. If the neighborhood is especially low-income, consider creating a weekly food give-away. Many times, local food banks have the food but not enough volunteers to get it to all the people or neighborhoods that really need it. Any event that will create an opportunity for dialog will work. This is the perfect time to have a booth with church information and invite people to your church.

There's no need to reinvent the wheel here. If you already know of good Christian-based ministries or reputable agencies working in your area, consider partnering with them. Many times these agencies are doing many of the things mentioned above, but they may be lacking the volunteers to accomplish everything they have planned. This can create a wonderful opportunity for your church to contribute manpower to a project. In this way you are working with the agency, not duplicating their ministry or competing with it.

If you are going to contribute to or work with local agencies, it's important to establish some criteria for establishing partnerships with local and national ministries and community-based organizations. These can range from nonprofits that provide services to your local communities, national organizations, and ministry organizations in either of the categories mentioned previously. The definition of partners should be based on reciprocal relationships—the type of relationship that provides benefit to both organization and church in advancing each other's mission and vision. These organizations should exist for the public benefit, with the highest level of integrity in your community. Below is a set of criteria your team should consider before partnering with an agency or organization.

Missions-Minded Church
Local Ministry and Community Based Organization Criteria for Partnership

The following criteria are meant to serve as a basic guideline for developing a partnership for either a local or national ministry, or a nonprofit, for-public-benefit organization.

1.) Has integrity in mission, vision, operations, and reputation.

2.) Is proven to make a difference in their respective communities and foster goodwill and networking relationships with other like organizations.

3.) Is a legal entity with proper documents that guarantee its nonprofit status, locally and nationally, as a religious or for-public-benefit organization.

4.) Is willing to work with MMC to impact the human condition for the common good and meet similar doctrinal beliefs or statements of faith (if the partner is a ministry organization).

5.) Commits to providing monthly activity reports or at least quarterly updates.

6.) Commits to responding to the MMC GMT each year for continued support.

7.) If a ministry organization, holds a statement of faith which is in substantial agreement with MMC's statement of faith (separate from #4).

8.) Has a diversified governing board in which the chairperson and chief executive officer are different people, and authority and accountability are clear.

9.) Submits its most recent annual financial statement as proof of good stewardship.

10.) Submits a statement of its practices or policies under which it operates.

11.) Would be more effective serving a particular community need than MMC could do on its own, or whose partnership could enhance a ministry that MMC currently offers.

12.) The ministry or organization does not use more than 15% of its total annual operating budget on overhead.

Many projects are too large for any one church to complete by itself. When this happens, consider combining your resources (both people and finances) to make a positive, visible impact on the people and neighborhoods in your city or town. For this to work, each church has to get over any fear it might have of either church stealing potential flock. Unfortunately, some churches do think this way. The idea should be to give Jesus a great reputation in your city. When churches work together unselfishly, great things happen!

Once you become comfortable with this idea, consider starting a Christian Community Impact Network of churches that work toward creating a visible Christian presence in your community. A network can make a positive impact by addressing needs that the city or nonprofit organizations identify. By combining each church's individual strengths, you have a greater possibility of attracting the attention and gaining the respect and admiration of your community and its leaders.

Creating a network also means building a vehicle that gives all participating churches access to the same information at the push of a button. The network could act as a conduit of information for available projects to participate in. You could create a list of projects, with each project detailing the financial and human participation need. Every church that chooses to partner and participate in the network will be providing a service to your community.

Being a part of a recognized network can sometimes provide greater visibility with community leaders. As a network of Christian churches, you would be able to work with community leaders to select and prioritize community projects. Because every church has different strengths, different churches could take leadership roles on different projects, but with every church that wishes participating in that particular project.

It's important that individual member churches remain nameless with the public (outside of city leaders) so that there is no risk of it looking like a particular church is trying to use a project to build their own flock. Of course, each church has the option of taking on smaller projects themselves if they choose to—in fact, the more, the better.

If done properly, a network can build relationships between the Christian community, civic leaders, and communities in your city or town. It can become a resource network for pastors, city leaders, community leaders, and organizations. A network can help identify strengths and needs of current member churches. It can also serve to help smaller churches with things like building repairs or offering specific ministry services to their members, on their premises, that they may not be able to provide on their own.

The key is to make sure the network isn't duplicating the current efforts of existing organizations. You also want to make sure that you prioritize projects in a rational manner to avoid excessive burden on members of the network. You want to be able to complete the projects you are involved with in a manner that truly blesses the recipients and allows for the greatest impact. You also want to make a point to reach out to local Christian churches of other cultures so that no nationality of the Christian community is left out, and all have knowledge and access to the network.

These are just a few ideas to help you get your members involved in outreach. When you boil it all down to its purest form, missions is God finding people who are right with Him and placing them where they can make a difference for His kingdom. Jesus taught his disciples in Matthew 5:15–16:

> *You are the light of the world. A city on a hill cannot be hidden. Neither do people light a lamp and put it under a bowl. Instead they put it on its stand, and it give light to everyone in the house. In the same way, let your light shine before men, that they may see your good deeds and praise your Father in heaven.*

Your team has a responsibility to help the people of your congregation and the churches of your community to be that shining light.

CHAPTER 10

▼

DEFINING SUCCESS

The previous chapters of this book have hopefully given you some tools to build and improve your missions program with more Strategic Intent. But once implemented, how do you decide when they are successful? One church's idea of success might be completely different from another. Obviously, there should be signs of the ministry bearing fruit. But have you raised the bar high enough to really challenge your team and improve your program? And how often are you monitoring the progress and results of your missions program?

Webster's Dictionary defines success as "a favorable result." It defines successful as "turning out as was hoped for." Is your missions program being blessed with favorable results? Are things turning out as you had hoped for? Until you define success, you have nothing to aspire to. In order to measure success, you have to ask yourself three very important questions:

1. How do we define success?

2. What type of timeline are we going to implement?

3. If we are successful in meeting our goals, what will our church look like?

The success your missions program achieves will be in direct proportion to the quality of the goals you set and the type of commitment you give them. In business, the public usually makes sure a company ultimately gets what it deserves. I hate to say it, but it's not that different in ministry. If you want your program to be more successful, then you have to do more to deserve it. God honors people and ministries that work for His purposes:

> *I the Lord search the heart and examine the mind, to reward a man according to his conduct, according to what his deeds deserve.* (Jer. 17:10)

I created *Strategic Intent* to help missions teams set, manage, and achieve goals that are specific, measurable, trackable, and Spirit-led. The more specific a goal is, the easier it is to focus on it, and the more likely it will be achieved. Goals need to be set up in such a way that the results they produce (or lack of them) can be measured. If a goal isn't set up so it can be measured, then it shouldn't be a goal. Some goals fade from memory after they are achieved. So make sure your goals are trackable and can keep building on themselves. The goal should either have the effect of reproducing itself over and over again, or trigger the achievement of other related goals.

Anyone can go about the task of setting goals, but they should be created only after some serious time in prayer and a direct sense of God's leading. Goals should contribute to the overall success of your missions program if they are achieved. A ministry can achieve tons of goals, but they don't mean anything if they don't add up to something when all is said and done. It's like the quarterback of a football team who looks at his stats at the end of a season with pride and says to his coach, "Wow, look at that. My attempt-to-completion ratio is fantastic, and I didn't throw any interceptions all year." And the coach replies, "Yeah, but we didn't win any games either." It doesn't matter how many passes you complete if they don't lead to some touchdowns and help win some games.

Before you start setting a bunch of new goals with your team, God has to give you a vision of the future of your program if you achieved those goals. When you envision the future of your missions program, you need to be in alignment with God's will and also think without limitations. Why is this so important? Because God doesn't have any limitations. 1 Samuel 14:6 teaches us that "nothing can hinder the Lord." There's a job to be done, and we shouldn't put limitations on how God might use us for his purposes.

The goals you are led toward should be clear and compelling, and serve as a unifying focal point for your team to rally around. They should have clear finish lines so the ministry knows when it has achieved the goals. They might require thinking beyond the current capabilities of your ministry and current environment. They might (and probably should) require extra effort, extra faith and perhaps a little extra risk to achieve. But God instructs us to be bold in 1 Chronicles 22:13:

Be strong and courageous. Do not be afraid or discouraged.

The ministry vision God places on your heart and in your mind should be easily described to others whether in person or on paper. If someone were to look at your missions program in five to ten years, what would they see? Your ministry vision is all about translating the description to words and pictures; in essence, you are creating an image for what people will see.

Does it contain passion, emotion, and conviction? Does it rely on faith in God? Your ministry vision should describe what the ministry will look like and what it will feel like to members of your team and church if it is achieved. Remember that it is creation, not prediction.

The ministry vision that God gives you should get your juices flowing, be stimulating, spur forward momentum, and get your team going. Some of you reading this might be uncomfortable sharing your passion about the dreams that God has planted in your heart, but it's that passion and ability to share emotion that will attract and motivate others. You should be able to describe things like: What will your team be doing to help fulfill the great commission? What is your ministry's primary role? How will others see your ministry? I'll give you an example:

> We will be a church where our excitement and passion to serve Christ will be obvious for anyone to see and contagious for everyone to catch because of a missions program that has equipped and released people that God has gifted with various gifts, talents, abilities, and personalities to participate in the growth of this ministry for His kingdom.

> We will be actively sought by our peers to help equip their ministries and share the success of our missions program because of the way we have successfully sought out and partnered with gifted and able-bodied missionaries, local Christians, and ministries worldwide who have a vision to change their nations.

> Because of our efforts, the church in unreached and persecuted countries will be growing faster and stronger than in areas where Christianity is practiced openly because MMC helped equip them. Through MMC, they will have found the hope, peace, and joy of a personal relationship with Jesus Christ, which gives them their passion to share the Gospel in unprecedented numbers.

We will place a great priority in investing in ministries that are able to help people in humanitarian ways, using food, clothing, medical equipment, and other supplies to share the love of Christ and create an opportunity to be an agent of change for the sake of the Gospel. Our church members, the ministries we partner with, and the people we are reaching for Christ will feel like our missions team has contributed to their life and the cause for Christ in a positive way.

Your ministry vision can be longer (well, not too much longer) or shorter than this example; it's completely up to you. The main point is that it is long enough to capture the essence of what your ministry is all about when you achieve the goals God has set for you. Once you have your vision and goals, then start planning with your team on how you might achieve them. Of course, all plans should be rooted in deep prayer. Remember to "commit to the Lord whatever you do and your plans will succeed." (Prov. 16:3) Because the actions you take now will send ripples through future generations.

So now we go back to the original question of this chapter: How do you define success? As discussed earlier, success can be defined many different ways. We need to create a level playing field with common denominators that every missions program could agree to. What better place to find those common denominators than in the Holy Bible?

When the apostle Paul wrote to the church in Corinth, it was rife with divisions and problems, and many in the church refused to change for its betterment. In his second letter, he gave them clear instructions on how they were supposed to conduct themselves:

> *So we make it our goal to please Him, whether we are at home in the body or away from it. (2 Cor. 5:9)*

As individuals, we could define this by judging our ability to please God at home, in the church body, and away from it. If we carry this school of thought to the church, we could define this by a missions program's ability to please God in the church, in the community, and in the world. I would then pose the question, "Is your church a healthy church, a harvest church, and a holistic church? What role is your missions program playing in helping your church to have those attributes?" Here is how I would define those attributes:

A Healthy Church, Focuses *IN* (internal signs of health and personal transformation)

A Harvest Church, Focuses *OUT* (evangelism and un-reached people groups)

A Holistic Church, Focuses *THROUGH* (community impact and societal transformation)

Ask yourself the following questions:

Is your church a Healthy Church? Are the majority of members growing in their faith and being discipled? Are they inviting friends to church? Are church members consistently exposed to missions education opportunities? Is missions being taught in the children's ministries? Do the majority of members have an awareness of your missions program and ministry partners? Are you continuing to see more members become involved in your missions program? Is at least half the church congregation regularly praying for your ministry partners? Have all of your small groups adopted a ministry partner to lift up and pray for each week? Are at least half of the team members on short-term trips each year first-timers? Is your missions budget growing each year?

Is your church a Harvest Church? How many people are coming to Christ as a result of your missions program each year? How many lives are being changed? Do the majority of your funds go toward funding ministry partners and projects in unreached countries? Are you funding ministries that have the ability to multiply themselves into a church planting movement? Is the amount of ministry partners or church planters you support increasing each year? Are the amount, size, and scope of projects you fund increasing each year? Has your church adopted an unreached people group? Is your missions program gaining attention because of it success in the missions field?

Is your church a *Holistic* Church? Are you seeing a positive impact in your local community as a direct result of your missions program? Do you have programs that address the homeless, the hungry, the poor, and the less educated? Are people's lives being changed because of your involvement with them? Are you specifically reaching out to other nationalities within your community? Is the local community aware of your church? Does it view your church in a positive light? Do you network with other churches in order to make a greater impact on the local community? Do civic leaders seek your church's opinions on community projects?

The "S" Factor

All of the above items are great ways to measure if your church or missions team is achieving the results God intended for you. But ultimately, you have to ask yourself these five all-important questions:

How many lives have been **S**aved?

How many people have been **S**erved?

How many people have been **S**chooled? (discipled)

How many people have been **S**ent?

How much has the Gospel been **S**hared?

It's what I call "The 'S' Factor." Those of us who have a personal relationship with Jesus Christ must remember that we were blessed to be a blessing. We were saved to help save others, saved to serve, saved to school, saved to send, and saved to share. We have a responsibility to equip fellow believers to do the same. If a church and its members can be equated to growing a tree, we have to help that tree grow deep roots and produce healthy, fruit-bearing branches.

Instead of churches asking how can we grow, we should be asking, how can we save, how can we serve, how can we school, how can we send, how can we share? So how are you doing? What is your "S" Factor?

It all has to start with the saving part. If you work toward that goal, everything else will fall into place. It's really quite that simple. When you sift through personal opinions, strong emotions, and church politics, that's what it's all about. Because in its simplest form, missions is God finding people who are right with Him and placing them where they can make a difference for His kingdom. For it is by acts, not by ideas, that people achieve. Too many missions programs are mired in mediocrity and led by pastors, team leaders, or church leaders who are content with the way things are. But when contentment sets in with the way you do your job, progress stops, and the rest of the world suffers.

The writer of Proverbs 24:30–34 explains what will happen to a ministry that is underperforming, not seeking to improve itself, or operating with a general lack of urgency:

> *I went past the field of the sluggard, past the vineyard of the man who lacks judgment; thorns had come up everywhere, the ground was covered with weeds and the stone wall was in ruins. I applied my heart to what I observed and learned a lesson from what I saw: A little sleep, a little slumber, a little folding of the hand*

to rest—and poverty will come on you like a bandit, and scarcity like an armed man.

The greatest reward for doing something well is the opportunity to do more. There are no shortcuts to any place worth going. Is your missions program going somewhere? Where does it fall in the scheme of things? Are you and your team obeying the plans God has laid out for your ministry? How would you rate yourself and what kind of a grade would you give your team? Does your team trust you as their leader? Do you support and encourage them to work together in a spirit of unity to achieve the team's goals?

Are you and your team continually striving to improve your program? Do you and your team attend conferences and seminars to learn and share new ideas? Are you aware of what other missions programs are accomplishing and, more importantly, how they are accomplishing it? Are you and your team following God's leading or the leading of other churches? It's good to beware of what other churches are doing, but you need to be careful of what you compare yourself to.

In the last century, great strides have been made to evangelize the world for Christ. The techniques and paradigms that were incorporated during that period brought much success, but the church in America can't rest on its laurels. As the world changes, new techniques must be used, and new paradigms must be incorporated. The reality we have to face is that what worked before isn't working so well anymore. We have to change our way of thinking. We have a responsibility to make the most with what God gives us and we must not abdicate that responsibility.

Jesus was a strategic thinker. He adapted his strategy to each unique situation He encountered. He had no one-size-fits-all missions approach. He said different things to different people and responded differently to each person. His message never changed, just his approach. His main concern was to be understood, so He adapted his approach based on each individual's needs or personal reality. If Jesus did this, than we should strive to adapt to a changing world, too. Our message doesn't need to change, just our approach.

We still face the challenge of reaching people who live in places where few people have yet to hear the Gospel. We still face the challenge of helping more members in our churches acquire the desire to help complete the Great Commission. We still face the challenge of creating a church environment where people are actually excited to attend on Sunday mornings. And we still face the challenge of creating a church that is making a positive impact on the rest of society and can be seen making a positive difference in peoples lives.

The hour has come for the church in America to wake up from its slumber. It's time to act with a greater sense of urgency and help the members of our churches to discover and utilize the gifts and talents that God has so mightily blessed them with so they can be salt and light to the rest of the world. As missions leaders, we have the unique opportunity and responsibility to play a strategic role in helping the world know our Lord and Savior Jesus Christ. If we do our job well, God will be glorified, and the world will be blessed.

Psalm 67

May God be gracious to us and bless us
And make his face shine upon us;
May your ways be known on earth,
Your salvation among all nations.
May the peoples praise you, O God;
May all the peoples praise you.
May the nations be glad and sing for joy,
For you rule the peoples justly
And guide the nations of the earth.
May the peoples praise you, O God;
May all the peoples praise you.
Then the land will yield its harvest,
And God, our God will bless us.
God will bless us,
And all the ends of the earth will fear Him.

Amen.

For more information about Strategic Intent Ministries,

please visit our Web site, www.strategicintent.org.

978-0-595-50543-2
0-595-50543-0

Printed in the United States
203037BV00002B/103-150/P